T0090803

A Unique Walk

Kaylee with Shirley Hildebrandt

authorHOUSE®

AuthorHouse™
1663 Liberty Drive
Bloomington, IN 47403
www.authorhouse.com
Phone: 833-262-8899

Published by AuthorHouse 01/18/2022

ISBN: 978-1-6655-4836-6 (sc)
ISBN: 978-1-6655-4835-9 (e)

Library of Congress Control Number: 2022900301

Print information available on the last page.

Image credit to Audrey Harris Photography

All scripture quotations are from The Holy Bible, English Standard Version® (ESV®). Copyright ©2001 by Crossway Bibles, a division of Good News Publishers. Used by permission. All rights reserved.

This book is printed on acid-free paper.

CONTENTS

FOREWORD

Fifteen years ago, my path was forever changed, and I believe yours will be as well after reading this book. This is the story of my granddaughter, Kaylee, who suffers from severe cerebral palsy. It is a look inside the life and mind of a beautiful, creative, funny, and loving young woman who lives daily with disability. The pages of this book were written by her in thought and in practice.

Cerebral palsy is a neurological condition caused by brain damage usually before or during birth. Cerebral palsy causes a range of disabilities, from mild to severe. Each child has a unique and individual experience with cerebral palsy. Some potential issues include movement and walking disabilities, speech difficulties, learning disabilities, cognitive impairments, hearing or vision loss, epilepsy, emotional and behavioral challenges, spinal deformities, and joint problems. There is no cure.

Kaylee came to me several years ago, saying, "I want to write a book about my life. Will you help me?" I find it important to share with you the process used in writing this book. Kaylee is a very intelligent young lady. She reads well and understands concepts and thoughts better than most her age. But she is limited, due to her cerebral palsy, in expressing those thoughts because of her inability to speak clearly so that others can comprehend. She also has very limited hand control, so she is unable to write.

The writing of this book consisted of me sitting down with Kaylee, allowing her to talk and answer questions. I would type her responses onto my computer, and then she would copy what I had typed onto her computer.

She would type one letter at a time, using one finger at a time. She was insistent upon typing as much as she physically could. This process took hours to complete one paragraph. What seemed, at times, a daunting task to me was one she was overjoyed to perform. She daily asked, "Are we going to work on my book today?"

So, letter by letter, page by page, this is the story of a young woman's courage and sorrow with cerebral palsy. But, oh, it is *so* much more! It is a story of hope, purpose, and beauty inside the world of disability. A story that values the ordinary, or dare we say, broken, and shows there is joy in Christ in all things. A story that describes a path unique to her yet filled with lessons for us all as we walk our designated paths.

At sixty-three years of age, I have taken a few steps in my life, many wandering in different directions, many times falling down and getting back up, and even some in the right direction. As a believer in Jesus Christ, I have found it best to follow His lead.

While helping Kaylee write this book, I was humbled many times by her responses and thoughts. I can recall several times at the end of our sessions, going into my room, shutting the door, and crying, asking God to forgive me for my selfishness. There were also times she and I laughed so hard we cried. Listening to her story taught me so many lessons and helped me to focus on what is truly important in life. While reading this book, you will hear Kaylee's story, and then at the end of each chapter, I will share what I have learned and perhaps what we all can learn from her walk.

I invite you to walk down this path with Kaylee. It is a road less traveled. It is a unique walk. It is not a walk that Kaylee chose, nor her parents, nor her family. Nevertheless, it is a walk chosen for her by God. It is uniquely hers, and Christ is leading the way.

—Shirley Hildebrandt

PREFACE

The reason I am writing this book is so that you will enjoy your life and learn to be happy. I am learning how to be happy by following Jesus's example. I love my life, but at times, it is very hard for me. Even though it is hard, following Jesus helps me to be strong. This book is the story of my life and how I am learning to live with cerebral palsy. It is a story about my unique walk.

CHAPTER 1

I AM UNIQUE

On July 28, 2006, my mom had a miracle, and it was me. My mom's name is Bethany. She fought really hard for me to live. I was born with cerebral palsy, so I must be a strong girl. Sometimes I wonder why I was born with cerebral palsy, but I think it is because God made me special and wanted me to show how strong He is. God makes us all special. We all look different on the outside, but we are all beautiful to Him.

My birth was very difficult and scary. My mom was at home, and she passed out when she went into labor with me. My dad was at home and called the ambulance. My mom lost a lot of blood, so the doctor had to give her several transfusions. A transfusion is when the doctor gives you blood that someone has donated in order to save your life. My mom was taken by helicopter to DeKalb Medical Center in Atlanta.

I rode in a special ambulance. She wanted me to be with her at that hospital. I was in the hospital for seven days, watched and taken care of by many nurses and doctors.

When I went home from the hospital, no one knew I had cerebral palsy. Everyone knew I had a rough birth but thought I was fine. They were all just happy that I was alive and that Mom was alive too.

My parents worked very hard to get me to eat so I would grow. I could not suck from a bottle and had a hard time eating from the very beginning. My mom told me that she would put breast milk in a little syringe, tilt my head back, and then put the drops of milk into my throat. She would blow on my face so that I would swallow. This is how I was fed. It took a long time just to swallow a little bit of milk. They weighed me every day to make sure I was gaining weight. When I was a baby, the doctors diagnosed me with "failure to thrive." I was put in the hospital for a few days so they could make sure I was getting enough food. I also had acid reflux and cried a lot.

I did not roll over on time, and I did not sit up on time or learn to crawl when other babies did. I finally learned to crawl, and though it was different from how most babies crawled, I was able to move, and crawling was how I moved around for many years.

Everything was difficult for me, and my mom, dad, and family knew it. They spent many hours praying for me and caring for me. I was different from the beginning. I am sure that my mom and dad worried about me all the time. I know that they must have cried and felt very scared. I am so glad that they knew Jesus and that He helped them make it through the hard days.

At nine months, I had an MRI, and my parents were told that I had cerebral palsy—specifically, spastic quadriplegia, a severe form of cerebral palsy that prevents me from controlling and using my legs, arms, and body. Basically, I can't use my whole body.

All of what I have written so far I don't remember, of course. My parents and grandparents have told me this part of my story. But I knew from the beginning God was with me. I could feel His love for me in my heart, and my parents knew He was with me too.

SHIRLEY HILDEBRANDT: Thinking back to when Kaylee was born is, quite honestly, painful. There was so much fear and uncertainty. There were many unanswered questions. Yet we had been given this beautiful little baby girl who had survived such a traumatic birth.

There are times in life when everything stops. The amount of money you possess, the success you have achieved, the grand plans you aspire to—none of these are given a second thought in times of deep pain. What I find we search for and rely on is our faith. It is where we go to find strength.

As we sat in the emergency room, we could hear cries of distress coming from inside as Kaylee was being born into the world. All we could do was cry ourselves. We cried to the Lord. He was the one we turned to.

The fear was strong, but we knew Christ was stronger. We also knew He was giving us the strength to rely upon Him.

Her mother and father did not plan this path for their firstborn child. This was not the path we, her family, had planned either. Yet this is where all our feet landed. Our eyes could not see what was before us. Hard as we tried, our minds were unable to comprehend what the future would hold. Our plans were changed. All we could do was trust and take one step at a time.

Isn't this how we find ourselves often in life, on a path or in a situation that is totally out of our control? As best we can, we try to navigate and see what is ahead, but more often than not, we cannot. It is so easy to rely on ourselves to try to fix the problem or change the course.

God's ways are higher than our ways. The path He designates for us is the path that is best. Even when we don't understand and we feel lost along the way, we must choose to trust that God will guide us.

> For you formed my inward parts; you knitted me together in my mother's womb. I praise you, for I am fearfully and wonderfully made. Wonderful are your works; my soul knows it very well. My frame was not hidden from you, when I was being made in secret, intricately woven in the depths of the earth. Your eyes saw my unformed substance; in your book were written, every one of them, the days that were formed for me when as yet there was none of them. How precious to me are your thoughts, O God! How vast is the sum of them! (Psalm 139:13–17)

> Trust in the Lord with all your heart; and do not lean on your own understanding. In all your ways acknowledge Him and He will make straight your paths. (Proverbs 3:5–7)

CHAPTER 2

MY FAMILY

I want to tell you about my family. My parents were married for almost two years before I was born. They got married on September 18, 2004. I am the firstborn in my family.

I have a little brother, Samuel, who is in heaven with Jesus now. It makes me sad that I never got to see him, but one day I will.

I also have a little brother who is six years old. His name is Eli Thomas. He is named after my great-grandpa, Thomas Howse. Eli goes to school now and is very smart. He learned to read and is the best reader in his class. He took tae kwon do for a while and was really good at that. I liked watching him at his competitions. Now he likes baseball.

Eli has always taken care of me. He opens doors for me when I am in my wheelchair, and sometimes he feeds me. He understands me when I talk, and he helps others to understand me too. When I need something, I can ask him to get it for me, and he will. Sometimes he gets me mad, though, especially when he argues with me. But I don't like to see him get into trouble. It upsets me when he does.

My baby sister's name is Madilyn Claire. We call her Madi or Moosie. Everyone said she was the best baby they had ever seen. She really was. When she was little, I would get on the floor and play with her. I can't do that now. She is three years old now and plays with Eli all the time. I love watching her play and run around our house. I think when she is older, we will be really good friends.

I love my brother and sister so much. They make a lot of noise running around the house. So much noise sometimes causes me to have anxiety, but I am working on trying not to let it bother me.

Let me tell you a little about my dad. His name is Josh, and he is a pastor at Highview Church in Villa Rica, Georgia. He is an awesome preacher and worship leader. He helps people with their problems and prays with them. He has taught me to sing. I have been singing with him since I was three. Sometimes when I have anxiety about my cerebral palsy and my life, Dad and I sing worship songs together. Singing helps me to get my mind off my problems and to think about Jesus. Plus, I love spending time with my dad. He understands everything about me. I think it helps both of us.

My dad and I are a lot alike. I am creative just like him. I love when my dad talks to me about Jesus. We spend lots of time just talking about God and my cerebral palsy. I always feel so much better after talking with him.

My dad is also very funny. One day when my sister, Madi, was still a baby, she was in her infant seat, and my dad made me think he was throwing her up in the air really high. But he was actually using a baby doll instead. It scared me at first, but then it made me laugh so hard.

My mom is beautiful, and she takes great care of us. Her name is Bethany. She loves Disney, everything Disney. She plans a trip to Disney for us because she knows we love it. She knows that Disney is a place I can go with my family and have a good time, even though I am disabled.

She loves to sell Norwex, and she is really good at it. She keeps our house clean and nice. She used to work at the hospital, too, as a radiologist technician. She also helps my dad at the church. My mom always makes sure that I get all the things I need. I know she will always take care of me.

I love my grandparents and all my family. I have lots of aunts, uncles, and cousins. I feel loved by all of them.

I like being the firstborn because I am the oldest. I can remember things. I help take care of my little brother and sister by letting my parents know if they need them. I talk to them and keep them company, and sometimes we watch videos together. But I wish I could play outside and run around with Eli and Madi. I wish I could help my mom and dad clean the house. I wish I could cook dinner for my dad. I would love to help my family more, but most things I cannot do.

I am glad God gave me my family. They are the most important people in my life. I will always love them.

SH: There's nothing quite like family. Everyone has one. Everyone needs one. Our family is the foundation of who we are and to some extent who we become. Families provide acceptance, unconditional sacrifice, joy, support, and love.

The family is not an institution designed by humans. It was created by God for the benefit of humans, and humans have been given stewardship over it. To know and glorify God is the purpose of each individual within a family.

God places us within the family He designs for us. He is sovereign over all, even our birth order. God uniquely gifts the father and mother with everything they will need to raise each individual child. He places within their care a little heart that is to be molded and fashioned to understand and know who He is and value His love for them.

The love that Kaylee shared with me regarding her family was so touching. She is a young lady who experiences the world, in part, through the eyes, mind, and legs, if you will, of her family. When they experience joy that she cannot, she is happy. When they discover something new that she cannot enjoy, she is thankful and excited for them. The places they can physically walk, move, and explore, she, in part, comes along. This is not to say that she doesn't desire those experiences. We know she does. But it is to say that she loves in such a way that she is joyful in the good of others.

An example of this is the day she asked to be taken to the tree house. In the spring of 2020, her grandfather decided to build a tree house. He worked many weeks on it, putting in a slide, lots of swings, and a deck. From the tree house, a zip line was put in for all the grandkids to enjoy.

Kaylee watched from our front porch as he built it. The tree house was situated on the side of our yard, down a slope into the woods. It would be pretty difficult to manage her wheelchair down there. She knew that this was going to be a place of fun for her siblings and cousins.

The day arrived for all the grandkids to come play. They all showed up and had the best time. Kaylee sat on the front porch in her wheelchair, watching from a distance. She was happy and content. Weeks and weeks went by as the grandchildren continued to come and play.

One afternoon, several months later, Kaylee came over to visit all by herself. As we sat on the front porch together, she asked her Pop (grandfather), "Do you think you could walk me down to the tree house?" "I would like to just stand on the deck and look over it."

Pop lifted her out of her wheelchair, and slowly, step by step, she walked with him as he held her from behind to the tree house. They carefully climbed the steps to the deck together. At the top of the deck, she leaned against the railing and smiled a smile like only she can and said, "I do love this!" Her heart was content.

My heart was full as I watched her. Although she could not enjoy the tree house fully like her siblings or cousins, she was determined to enjoy what she could. Her disability did not limit her ability to love. She was not limited in her ability to find joy in the good of others. She was not limited in her ability to be thankful.

Oh, how I pray that I will find joy in the good of others. I want to love and serve those within my family for the glory of Christ. I want to rid myself of petty excuses not to serve. I want to choose thankfulness over ingratitude. I want to see those within my family as more important than myself.

I can do this with God's help as He shows me how to serve others and lay down my life for my family and friends.

I encourage you to look for ways to take joy in the good of another within your family and those around you. Ask God to give you strength and a desire to love others as He loves you.

> "This is my commandment, that you love one another as I have loved you. Greater love has no one than this, that someone lay down his life for his friends. You are my friends if you do what I command you. No longer do I call you servant, for the servant does not know what his master is doing; but I have called you friends, for all that I have heard from my Father I have made known to you. You did not choose me, but I chose you and appointed you that you should go and bear fruit and that your fruit should abide, so that whatever you ask the Father in my name, he may give it to you." (John 15:12–17)

> Do nothing from selfish ambition or conceit, but in humility count others more significant than yourselves. (Philippians 2:3)

Kaylee and Dad

Kaylee and Mom
(Photo Credit: Audrey Harris, Audrey Harris Photography)

Kaylee with family (Bethany, Josh, Kaylee, Madi and Eli)
(Photo Credit: Audrey Harris, Audrey Harris Photography)

Kaylee at top of treehouse

CHAPTER 3

THERAPY

At first, there was hope that I might one day walk. I had a little walker and special braces for my legs. A therapist came to my house when I was small and worked with me. As I got older, I went to therapy, and they worked to help me walk. I wore a special suit that helped with my balance. The therapists would tie bungee cords to a vest on my body and use these cords to help me balance and stand up. I even rode a horse as part of my therapy. Her name was Snowflake. I loved riding Snowflake. Riding her made me feel happy and free.

The doctors and therapists told my parents that if I didn't learn to walk by the age of seven, I probably never would. I didn't know this until my parents told me. I'm sure every day that I wasn't getting better and stronger made them so sad. I know they wanted me to walk. When I turned seven, I could not walk. Now, I am in a wheelchair. This is how I get around. I have a power wheelchair that I can drive.

Therapy is a big part of my life. I have physical therapy, occupational therapy, and speech therapy. Seems like I have always had therapy. I have had many years of therapy. I still go today. I go to get stronger and to keep my muscles from stiffening up. I have always loved going to therapy. I love doing the work and seeing my therapists. They are kind and patient with me, always telling me I am strong. When I am at therapy, I do lots of different exercises. These exercises stretch my legs and arms.

Therapy has changed for me over the years. When I was little, I can remember practicing to walk with leg braces, and I used a walker. I used to work at getting into a position on my knees, and I would "knee walk."

This is how I learned to get around for many years. I also could sit on the floor. But as I have gotten older and bigger, I am no longer able to move around on my knees. I miss being able to get on my knees and sit alone on the floor. When Eli, my brother, was a baby, I could sit on the floor and play with him, but I am unable to do that now.

This is what a day of therapy looks like for me now. When I first get there, I lie on a soft red mat and work my ankles. I roll my ankles to warm up. My therapist helps me do this. Then I work on my arms. I am placed on the floor, and I push up from the floor to a sitting position. This helps my arms get strong. It is a lot of work for me. It is not easy.

I walk on a treadmill to strengthen my legs. My therapist puts a special belt on me and bungee cords. These help me to stand on the treadmill. I work to keep my balance so I can walk. I like this. I also stand on a machine, and it shakes my whole body to vibrate my muscles. Some days, my therapist leans me against a wall in the corner, and I stand for as long as I can and hold my balance. When I am able to stand up like that, after having to sit in my wheelchair all the time, I feel free. I am doing something all on my own, and I like that. So, when my therapist puts me in the corner, it's not because I've been bad. She puts me there because she knows I enjoy it and it helps me.

Since I can't run and play like other kids, my muscles do not get used. My muscles are always tight and stiff. So, therapy helps me use my muscles. It is kind of like play for me but not really. Other kids can climb trees, ride bikes and skateboards, and run and chase one another. But I can't do any of those things. So, I decided that when I go to therapy, to pretend like I am playing. It is a lot of work, and I get tired, but it is still fun, and I am glad I get to go.

One of my favorite parts of therapy is getting to talk with my therapists. We talk about whatever we want, and I love talking and listening to her. She is nice to me, and she loves the Lord. I look forward to seeing her every time I go to therapy. I think I will be going to therapy for many years, maybe forever, so that my muscles get some stretching and exercise. I am hoping this will help me.

SH: As Kaylee shared with me about what she remembered and what she does during therapy, I was amazed, again, by her outlook on life. Her mindset is one of determination, hope, and choosing to find the good in her situation. Her words, "It is a lot of work, and I get tired, but it is still fun, and I enjoy it," reveal her mindset.

Kaylee's story is not to focus on how strong she is, although she is a strong young woman. Kaylee's strength comes from who she is and who she belongs to. She knows she is a daughter of God, and she knows that He gives her the power and ability to overcome. She has learned and is continuing to learn to depend on His strength and compassion daily in her life and to allow Him to calm her fears. Since her disability is totally out of her control, this is a vital lesson for her.

I find it is difficult to have godly character when things in my life seem out of my control. I think I can control much of what is happening to me and around me. I think we all do. We plan our days, years, life. We plan to graduate, go to college, get married, settle into a nice career, have kids, buy a house, stay healthy, go on a trip. So much of our life is planned (we think). We think we are in control and find a false comfort in that thinking. Yet we don't have ultimate control over our health, our safety, or our family. We don't get to choose whether we will have cancer or face the loss of a child. We aren't in charge, and we need not be. We have a God who is in charge. This calms my anxious heart.

Can you imagine not being in control of your own body? Never knowing what it is like for your legs to perform what your mind wants them to do. Never knowing what it is like to comb your own hair, run on the beach, put your socks on, ride a bicycle. The list goes on and on for Kaylee, as this is her life. She is, for the most part, not in control of her body. Cerebral palsy has taken that from her. She is out of control and learning how to deal with it on a daily basis. Yet she is in control of how she reacts to each circumstance, and she makes an effort to control her emotions and anxieties the best that her disability will allow.

When we feel out of control, it is best to choose to rest in God, for He is in control of all things. He is in charge of all circumstances, even those that cause us to fear. We don't choose the circumstances that make us feel out of control, but we do choose the way we react. Our reactions should exhibit an attitude of trust, hope, and rest. Trust in Christ that

He is present and all-knowing, kind, and good. Hope that He is working all things out for our good and His glory. And last but not least, rest … because as we trust and hope in Him, our hearts are stilled, and His peace satisfies like nothing else.

Whatever we face in this life, we can have hope knowing that God is in control. He is a good God, full of love, mercy, and compassion. John Piper says, "If God can be in control of the cross with all of its sin and all of its horror and pain, then he can be in control of our pain and horror." When we take our eyes off of our situation and focus on God, He directs us and gives us peace. We can have hope for the future because our hope is in God.

Our reactions to difficult situations can bring glory to God. We really can choose to find good in difficult things. We can, like Kaylee says, feel "happy and free."

> My thoughts are not your thoughts, neither are your ways my ways, declares the Lord. For as the heavens are higher than the earth, so are my ways higher than your ways, and my thoughts than your thoughts. (Isaiah 55:8–9)

> In Him we have obtained an inheritance, having been predestined according to the purpose of Him who works all things according to the counsel of His will. (Ephesians 1:11)

> But now thus says the Lord, he who created you, O Jacob, he who formed you, O Israel: "Fear not, for. I have redeemed you; I have called you by name, you are mine. When you pass through the waters, I will be with you; and through the rivers, they shall not overwhelm you; when you walk through fire you shall not be burned, and the flame shall not consume you." (Isaiah 43:1–2)

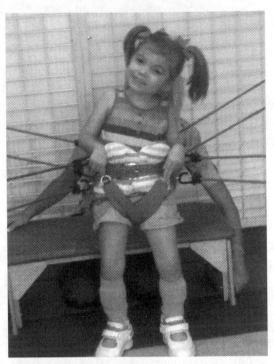

Kaylee at therapy using bungee cords 2011

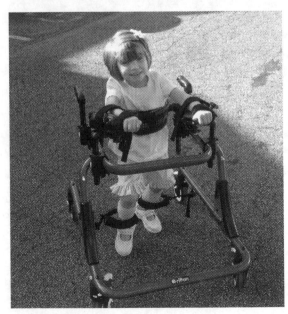

Kaylee in red walker 2011

Kaylee at therapy on treadmill 2013

Kaylee at therapy standing

CHAPTER 4

MY FAITH

When I was eight years old, I began to understand about what Jesus did for me on the cross. I have been taught my whole life about Jesus and how much He loves me. My parents have always taken me to church and told me about Jesus. I believe Jesus died for me, was buried, and rose from the grave. He sits beside God now in heaven. I wanted to be baptized so that other people would know that I believed in Jesus. My dad baptized me at Highview Church.

I was not scared at all to be baptized because I knew my dad would hold me and pull me up out of the water. All of my family were there. It was such a happy day for me. I wanted others to know that Jesus died on the cross for me. I choose to be happy in Jesus because He helps me. When I am afraid, He tells me it will be all right. When I can't walk or run like my friends, He tells me He understands and that one day I will walk and run and even dance. Jesus is my best friend. I can talk to Him anytime I want. He is never too busy to listen to me. He understands me. When I am overwhelmed with my cerebral palsy, I have to go to Him.

My dad tells me to trust Jesus, and I am learning how, little by little. I love to talk about heaven and being with Jesus. I want to have a new body one day and talk to God. When I get to heaven, the first thing I want to do is *run*. I want to run up to Jesus and give Him a big hug. When He sees me, I think He will smile really big and say, "Welcome home, Kaylee."

I believe in prayer because I use it all the time. Lots of people pray for me, and I know that it works. God hears all my prayers, and He answers them too.

I have been asked, "Wouldn't you like to be healed?" Part of me thinks yes, but I also think that Jesus wants me just like I am, so that others can see how strong He really is. I know there are things He wants me to do with my disability. So, I am OK with that.

I hope God will use my disability to help others to understand people with disabilities. I want people to understand people with disabilities and take time to know us. I want people to not be afraid to talk to me and listen to me. We may look like our lives do not matter, but our lives do matter. My life matters, and my faith matters too.

SH: Faith and hope are two great gifts. We know love is the greatest. First Corinthians 13:13 says, "Now these three remain: faith, hope and love. But the greatest of these is love." I used to think that faith and hope were the same thing. They are related but distinct. "Now faith is the assurance of things hoped for, the conviction of things not seen" (Hebrews 11:1). Faith is confidence in what we hope for. As a believer, I have faith in Jesus Christ. I believe what He said is true. I trust in His finished work on the cross and His resurrection for my salvation. I trust in His Word, and that leads me to have hope.

Hope involves something that is yet to be seen. Romans 8:24 says, "Hope that is seen is no hope at all. Who hopes for what they already have?" I have hope that one day I will see Christ. I have hope for His glorious return. To me, hope is having an attitude expecting something good to happen. Hope is a part of my faith that focuses on the future. I have hope that Kaylee will receive a new body and be able to do all those things that she has not been able to do in this life.

John Piper says, "Hope is a heartfelt, joyful conviction that our short-term future is governed by an all-caring God, and our long-term future, beyond death, will be happy beyond imagination in the presence of the all-satisfying glory of God."

Don't you love to be around people who have hope? I know I do. They encourage me and give me hope. To know that this life is more than just the here and now, to understand that it's not all about me is freeing. The whole purpose of our lives is to bring glory to God and to share His goodness with others. This can only be accomplished by believing He is glorious and He is good.

Everyone will suffer at some point. Knowing Jesus is what makes life worth living in the good times and in the difficult times. Knowing Jesus gives us hope during those times and in the days ahead. Who can we trust in those times? Who can we believe? Where does our hope come from?

One day while sitting at home with Kaylee, she asked me, "Are you thankful that I have cerebral palsy?" At first, I thought I misunderstood her. I questioned her as to whether I heard her right. I said, "Well, yes and no." I was quite honestly thrown off guard by her question. I knew that deep down, more of me was not thankful that she had cerebral palsy.

She immediately said, "Well, I think you should say yes, because I'm not hurting, and I'm happy."

My heart jumped inside of me as I listened to her. I then thought, *I'll just throw this question right back at you.* So, I asked Kaylee, "Are you thankful you have cerebral palsy?"

Her answer, "Yes I am. It is hard, but I love my life."

Her answer was full of hope. It has to be. How else could she give an answer like that? She has hope because she has faith. She has faith because Christ gave it to her. She believes that her disability is not in vain. She believes that there is purpose in it.

R. C. Sproul said, "In a real sense, hope is faith looking forward." It is encouraging to see Kaylee hope in the goodness of God. While Kaylee's legs refuse her the opportunity to run, her soul can run to her Savior's arms anytime. Hearing her talk about one day seeing Jesus and running up to Him gives me hope. I know her faith is in the one who will run toward her as she is running toward Him. I have faith that day will come, and I hope to see it.

> For by grace you have been saved through faith. And this is not your own doing; it is the gift of God, not a result of works, so that no one may boast. (Ephesians 2:8–9)

> Rejoice in hope, be patient in tribulation, and be constant in prayer. (Romans 12:12)

For I know the plans I have for you, declares the Lord, plans for welfare and not for evil, to give you a future and a hope. (Jeremiah 29:11)

And without faith it is impossible to please him, for whoever would draw near to God must believe that he exists and that he rewards those who seek him. (Hebrews 11:6)

I have been crucified with Christ. It is no longer I who live, but Christ who lives in me. And the life I now live in the flesh I live by faith in the Son of God, who loved me and gave himself for me. (Galatians 2:20)

May the God of hope fill you with all joy and peace in believing, so that you by the power of the Holy Spirit may abound in Hope. (Romans 15:13)

So we do not lost heart. Though our outer self is wasting away, our inner self is being renewed day by day. For this light momentary affliction is preparing for us an eternal weight of glory beyond all comparison, as we look not to the things that are seen but to the things that are unseen. For the things that are seen are transient, but the things that are unseen are eternal. (2 Corinthians 4:16–18)

The Lord takes pleasures in those who fear him, in those who hope in his steadfast love. (Psalm 147:11)

CHAPTER 5

THINGS I LIKE TO DO:
MY HOBBIES/TALENTS

I want to do or at least try many things, but I have to find things that I can do. One thing I love to do is paint. My grandmother (I call her "Manga") has a special shop at her house. We paint and create things together there.

It is hard for me to control my hand movements. My hands do not do what I want them to do. Manga wanted to help me with my painting. She said she was lying in bed one night, and this idea came to her. She could use painter's tape and mark off exactly where I was to paint. I would come up with an idea, and she would tape off my idea on the canvas. Then I would paint in the areas marked off for me by the painter's tape.

The first picture she taped off for me was the picture of a sunset. I painted it, and then once the tape was pulled off, I was so happy. I could see the design and what I had done. It was what I wanted to paint even though my hands wouldn't let me. The tape idea worked! Manga still has the very first picture I painted using the tape. It's a beautiful sunset. I called the painting *The Ending of a Perfect Day*.

I have painted lots of pictures on canvas using the painter's tape. It takes me a long time to paint one picture, usually several days. But I don't mind because when I am finished, I am proud of myself. I have my own Facebook page called "The Painter's Granddaughter." Some of my work is shown on my page.

I painted a picture of another sunset. This one had a cross on it too. When I went to hear my favorite worship singer, Chris Tomlin, I was able to have dinner with him. I wanted to give him the picture I painted. So, when we had dinner together, he came over to our table, and I gave him the picture I painted. He loved it, and I will never forget that day! He gave me a fist bump and said he loved it. He said he was going to put it up in his house. I hope he did. It made me really happy, and I felt like my paintings could make other people happy too.

I had an art show on July 20, 2019, at City Station in Carrollton, Georgia. Manga planned this for me, and it took a lot of work and time. It was a special day, and I wanted to look beautiful, so my grandmother "Nonnie" fixed my hair and put makeup on me. She is a hairdresser and usually does my hair. I love her so much. My mom bought me a new dress. It was a long blue dress with silver designs on it, and I had sandals to match.

All of my paintings were placed on easels and set on tables for people to see and buy. We had cake, punch, and other snacks. A friend from my church helped decorate and provided the refreshments. More than one hundred people came to my art show. All of my thirty-six paintings sold within thirty minutes. It took me a couple of years to paint thirty-six paintings, but they sold so fast. I was so excited. My family and friends were there and even lots of people that I didn't know. There were people from other states who came just to buy one of my paintings.

One painting was a picture of an ice-cream cone with strawberry, vanilla, and chocolate ice cream. I painted this on canvas for my friends that own an ice-cream shop. They came to my art show, and I gave them their painting. They were so happy, and they hung it in their ice-cream shop. It's called the Butter'dudder. They have the best ice cream and milkshakes. I love going there.

At my art show, I played a video showing how I paint using painter's tape to guide me. Everyone seemed to enjoy watching how I paint that way. One woman said that her son watched the video, and when he went home, he talked about me for a long time and asked his mom if he could learn to paint like me. She said he was so impressed by watching me paint that he said he thought he could learn to paint and draw too. This made me so happy.

There were several kids with disabilities like me who came to my art show. A couple kids came to the show in wheelchairs, and I didn't know who they were, but they said they had heard about me and wanted to see my art. I was so excited to see other kids there with disabilities like me. I was happy that I could encourage other kids with disabilities. It was good to feel special and to know I was not alone.

I painted a special picture for my parents. It was a surprise for them. I used a big canvas and painted a picture of clouds and a field of wildflowers. I used a sponge to paint the clouds and small hand strokes to make the stems of the flowers. Then I used a bunch of Q-tips tied together to make the little flower petals. I dipped the Q-tips in paint and then pressed them on the canvas. On the picture was a stencil with the words "It's so Good to be Home." I made this for my mom and dad because I love them so much and I love being at home. Being at home always makes me happy.

I also love to sing with my dad. I have been singing with him since I was like four. He teaches me the song, and we sing it together. I've sang "Amazing Grace," "10,000 Reasons," and the last song we did together was called "Raise a Hallelujah." We had a friend record it while we sang. It was so much fun. It is on my daddy's YouTube channel.

I have many things that I enjoy doing. I enjoy going out to eat and spending time with my family. I love going out to coffee with my Pop and Manga. I love going to Nonnie's house because she cuts my hair and we talk to each other. I love going out to eat seafood with Nonnie and Poppy too.

I love going to church and seeing all my friends. I love to sing in church and worship the Lord. I can't lift my arms all the way up to praise the Lord, but I can lift them as high as I can. I love it when my dad preaches. Sometimes he makes a joke when he is preaching. I love that! I love to hear him talk about me in his sermons. I think it makes everyone feel good to hear about how I am doing. I'm glad my dad is a preacher because he is always telling me about the Lord. This helps me to love Jesus more.

I like talking to my pastor too. His name is Pastor Chad. I remember asking him questions about God after he would preach. He would always sit down and talk to me. I know that he prays for me and my family. He encourages me, and I love him.

I have to find things that I can do. I have learned to like them. There are a lot of things I can't do, but I like the things I can do.

SH: In the beginning, God created. We are created in the image of God, and this is where our creativity comes from. We are created to create. I think everyone has the ability to create. The tricky part is finding out what you enjoy creating and what you are good at doing. The things we create should bring glory to God. I think creativity is an act of worship.

We are all gifted at certain things, and we all have the capability of learning new things. I remember waking up in the middle of the night with the idea of using painter's tape to help Kaylee paint. Several days before, she and I had tried to paint. She painted what she could, and I noticed the look on her face. I could tell her painting did not look the way she had envisioned it. I thought, *Is this just one more thing that she will not be able to do or enjoy?*

So when the painter's tape idea worked, we were both ecstatic. Kaylee knows full well what she wants a painting to look like. Her mind is full of creativity and ideas. It is a joy working with her and watching her try new ways of painting. She has used balloons, Q-tips, sponges, stencils, leaves … all kinds of objects to help create a painting.

She asked to have music playing many times as she painted, and I could see her relax and feel confident in her ability to create. What she loved most was the hope that her paintings would make others happy. The idea that others would see value in what she had created kept her painting. It was also a blessing to see her reap the rewards of all her hard work.

We are all gifted to create differently. Some love to paint, sing, write, or cook, while others love to teach, practice medicine, organize, cut hair, you name it. Of all the beautiful ways to create, the most rewarding aspect of creating is giving God glory. We are created for the glory of God, and we should strive in our creating to bring God glory. Westminster Catechism says, "Man's chief end is to glorify God, and to enjoy him forever." So sing for God's glory, paint for God's glory, cook for God's glory, teach for God's glory. When you do this, you help to open the eyes, hearts, and minds of others to see the goodness of God and His love for them. Our gifts and talents are a means to praise God and win unbelievers to Christ.

When was the last time you created something? Try creating something today. You will find much joy in creating. I promise. It may take work at first, and you may run into obstacles. But don't let obstacles stand in your way. Kaylee didn't. Plus, there's always painter's tape!

So, whether you eat or drink, or whatever you do, do all to the glory of God. (1 Corinthians 10:31)

For we are his workmanship, created in Christ Jesus for good works, which God prepared beforehand, that we should walk in them. (Ephesians 2:10)

O Lord, how manifold are your works! In wisdom have you made them all; The earth is full of your creatures. (Psalm 104:24)

And he had filled him with the Spirit of God, with skill, with intelligence, with knowledge, and with all craftsmanship, to devise artistic designs, to work in gold and silver and bronze, in cutting stones for setting, and in carving wood, for work in every skilled craft. (Exodus 35:31–33)

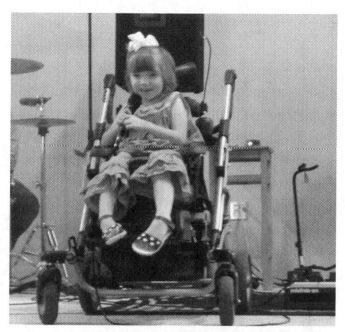

Kaylee singing at church. Six years old, May, 2012

Kaylee holding painting of sunset -
First painting using painter's tape

Kaylee Painting Cross

Kaylee sitting in front of her paintings

Kaylee at art show - July, 2019

Kaylee writing book sitting in front of computer

CHAPTER 6

SPECIAL TIMES

Birthdays for me are always fun. My mom makes sure they are special. She knows just how to plan a party. I've had all kinds of parties—princess party, luau party, Disney party.

One birthday I remember the most is my thirteenth birthday. My dad took me to the mountains. It was just him and me. We went out to eat, and we went to a wax museum. We also went shopping. I bought a pink hat, and my dad bought a hat too. I enjoyed spending time alone with my dad. We stopped and bought some candy on the way to the mountains and on the way back home! I can't eat just any candy. Some kinds are hard for me to chew and swallow. My favorite candy is Twizzlers. I can hold them, and they are easier for me to eat. We listened to a book in the van on the way, and we talked a lot too. I felt very special and loved that he would do that with just me.

When there is a special time planned, I always look forward to it. I get very excited and can hardly wait for that day to come. I talk about it over and over and over until the day finally comes. I want to know all the plans for the day too. I enjoy every minute of my special day, but once it is over, I can get sad really quickly. Sometimes it is difficult for me to process my emotions from one feeling to another. This is something that I am working on and have to ask Jesus for help. I ask Him to help me have a thankful heart and to stay calm.

I love going to Disney. My mom plans our trips, and we have a great time. Disney is a place I can go with cerebral palsy and still have a good time. I love all the shows at Disney, and I like most of the rides. I enjoy all the food too. I have a lot of good memories from going to Disney.

I want to tell you about this date that my dad and I went on. We went out to eat, and then we tried to think of something else to do. At first, we couldn't think of anything, and I was getting sad. Most things that I want to do, I can't. My dad asked me if I wanted to get my hair styled. I thought he was joking, like he always does. He wasn't joking, and I thought it would be fun. So, we went to Walmart ... of all the places. Walmart! My dad found a picture of a blonde hairstyle that we both liked. My hair is brown, and we decided that I would look great as a blonde.

He showed the picture to the stylist at Walmart and told her to make my hair look just like that. She started working on me. It took a really, really long time. I was tired of her working on my hair. When she finally finished, my hair was orange! Really orange! She knew it was orange, and my dad did too! So she worked on my hair even more. Some of the orange came out, but not all of it.

Once my hair was finished, I liked it. I looked like Marilyn Monroe. Dad and I went shopping and bought me some new clothes at Walmart too. After we left Walmart, we went home. My mom had *no idea* that my hair was now blonde. Da! Da! Da! When I got home, Dad took me into the bathroom to try on my new clothes. Mom did not see us go into the bathroom, and when we stepped outside, she saw my new blonde hair! My mom said, "What did you do?" She was not happy with my new hairstyle or my dad! My new hairstyle lasted about one week. I went to see Nonnie, and she worked her magic on me and fixed my hair.

After all that, I still loved my daddy-and-daughter date and will never forget it because my dad is so much fun!

SH: I loved hearing Kaylee tell me the story of her daddy-daughter date. We laughed so hard. She loves special days. Don't we all? I have found with Kaylee that if you tell her that you are going to do something with her, you better do it. I can understand this. For her, spending time with another person is what she enjoys most. She experiences much of life alongside others and through others. Just her knowing that you are going to spend time with her makes the day special to her. Her expectations are simple really. She just wants to spend time with you.

Time is one of the greatest gifts that God has given us. Giving someone your time is the best gift you can give them. Time is precious, and we all value our time. Yet we waste so much of it. I know I do. We make time for what we find most important. We accumulate planners and read blogs on how to manage our time. We make lists in order to manage our time and feel good about our busy lifestyles. We waste time trying to find time and perhaps even organize our time.

Spending time with the Lord helps me to be able to hear God's voice and see where He may be leading me to spend my time. It helps me to get my eyes off myself, my wants, and my desires and to see how I can invest my time wisely. The best use of your time starts with time alone with God. He is the author of time, and He knows how we should fill our days. I find it is best to spend time with the Lord at the start of my day. If I choose to leave Him out, then I'm probably not going to be making wise use of the time remaining in the day. When I choose not to spend time with God, my focus is off. I feel rushed, overwhelmed, and less productive. When I make the choice to spend time with God, I am able to set my mind on His purpose for the day. This settles my heart and causes me to rest, knowing He is planning my steps.

At the end of my life, I won't be concerned with what kind of home I lived in, or what type of car I drove, or which profession I held. I will be remembering and thankful for the time I spent with others. How is God calling you to use your time? You may need to say no to some things and yes to certain things that are most important. The good can be the enemy of the best.

I find that people who are truly hurting, for the most part, just want you to be there with them. Being present with someone in need has a healing effect. To sit beside them, listen to their need, and pray for them takes time. Those times are usually not marked on our to-do list. They just unfold in a given spot in time, and we have the opportunity to give what we have been given … the love of Christ and time. These opportunities unfold within our day, and the Spirit creates a time for us to be Jesus's hands and feet to someone. Oh, how I pray that I won't miss those opportunities.

You can turn someone's ordinary day into a special day just by giving the gift of your time.

> But seek first the kingdom of God and His righteousness, and all these thing will be added to you. (Matthew 6:33)

> So teach us to number our days that we may get a heart of wisdom. (Psalm 90:12)

> Be wise in the way you act toward outsiders; make the most of every opportunity. (Colossians 4:5)

> Look carefully then how you walk, not as unwise but as wise, making the best use of the time, because the days are evil. (Ephesians 5:15–16)

Kaylee at Disney with Mickey

CHAPTER 7

CEREBRAL PALSY HAS A STORY

I want to tell you about my life. I want to tell you my story so you can see what it is like for me every day. My cerebral palsy affects everything about my life. When I was a newborn baby, my mom worked so hard to make sure I was fed. She put milk in a little syringe and placed it in my mouth. I learned to swallow by my parents working on it with me over and over. The doctors told my parents, when I was a teenager, that it was because of their great care for me that I even learned to swallow and drink on my own. I have come a long way since then.

Someone usually always has to feed me. Sometimes, now that I am older, I can feed myself certain foods using a special bowl that has a suction cup on it to keep it in place on the table, and I use a spoon. At home, my mom and dad usually feed me. I always use a straw to drink with so that I don't choke. It's easier for me to drink with a straw. I love sweet tea and coffee. Some of my favorite foods are lasagna, macaroni and cheese, and seafood.

I love to eat, but sometimes it is frustrating for me because people have to feed me. I wish they knew to give me bigger bites! It is hard and easy at the same time. Hard because people have to have patience to feed me, and I have to have patience to let them do it their way. I get frustrated because I have to be patient and wait for them to give me the next bite.

Someone always takes me to the bathroom. They help me stand from my wheelchair, and while holding me up, we walk to the bathroom. I am able to move my legs with someone holding me up. I cannot stand by myself. This is why therapy has been so good for me, because I can at least move my legs and feet with help, even though I can't balance myself. I have always had someone (usually my parents and grandparents) take me to the bathroom, so I am used to it. Whenever I need to use the bathroom, they have to stop what they are doing to take care of me.

When I was younger, I would take baths. But since I am older and weigh more, it is harder to get me in and out of the bathtub. So, I take showers.

Where I am living now, I have a handicap shower. My parents worked hard and had a shower built just for me. I used some of the money that I made from my art show to help pay for my new handicap shower. I love it. My parents take me to the shower and sit me in a shower chair and leave me for a while to just let the hot water run on me to relax me. It feels good on my muscles. After a while, I call one of my parents back into the shower to bathe me. I am used to this too because I have never taken a bath or shower by myself.

My parents get me ready for bed. They put me in the bed and get me up every morning. My dad is always funny and makes me laugh at bedtime. He is always acting crazy. He is usually tired, and I think that is why he acts so crazy. Mom puts me to be bed sometimes too. They do not say prayers with me anymore because I am old enough to say my own prayers.

I like a fan going, and I need lots of blankets because I get cold at night. A lot of times, my blankets fall off, and I call for my parents in the night. I use pillows to help me too. They help when I lie on my side. It is hard for me to get comfortable sometimes. I call my parents to move me in a different position to help me. They come to my room and move me and arrange my pillows and blankets so I can get back to sleep.

I get anxious before I go to bed, and sometimes I have a really rough night. I am anxious about many different things. Sometimes it's because I need something and I can't get it by myself. I think, *What if someone breaks into my window and tries to take me and I can't scream loud enough? Or what if I fall out of my bed?* I am alone, but I have a monitor in my room so my parents can hear me. I try to go back to sleep. Sometimes I can, and sometimes I can't. If it is a really rough night, one of my parents will come into my room and help calm me down. They lie with me for a while, pray with me, and talk with me until I calm down and can go to sleep.

For a long time now, I have been getting headaches. I take different medicines for them. My parents took me to the eye doctor, and he gave me an eye exam and said I had very poor vision. So, I now wear glasses. I can see so much better with my glasses.

My dad took me to buy them. I have a strap on my glasses to help keep them on my head. My parents put them on me and take them off. At the end of the day, I am glad to get them off. They help me to see so much better, and I use my iPad every day, so I am very thankful to have my glasses.

I use an iPad a lot, and I am thankful for it. My iPad helps me in so many ways. It helps me to talk. I am glad I can use it to text people. I also have a program on it that helps me make sentences, and it speaks out loud so people can understand what I want to say. I can also FaceTime my family and friends. I watch videos and listen to music with it too. I love Christian worship music. My favorite songs right now are "He Will Hold Me Fast," "Good, Good Father," "I Raise a Hallelujah," "Yes, I Will," and my very favorite song is "Every Victory" by Danny Gokey.

I used my iPad to help write this book. Now that I am fifteen, I have my own Facebook page so I can stay in touch with my family and friends. I am not addicted to my iPad because I like to spend time with my family and friends more than being on my iPad.

My favorite show to watch is *The Chosen*. It is about the twelve disciples and Jesus. I have watched all the episodes several times. It also has an app that I downloaded, and I can watch the episodes any time I want. I have a *Chosen* T-shirt that says, "Get Used to Different," and I also have the *Chosen* devotional. They are going to be making several more seasons, and I can't wait to watch them when they come out.

I was taught at home for a few years when I was younger. Now I go to public school. I really enjoy going to school because I love to learn. I enjoy math. I use a big calculator to work out my math problems. I have several teachers who work with me. I have one teacher who stays with me the whole day. She helps me with my schoolwork, takes me to the bathroom, and helps me at lunchtime. Her name is Ms. Dana Bolton. She loves the Lord, and that makes me happy. She is not just my teacher; she is my friend.

I also enjoy reading. Sometimes I read, and other times my teacher reads to me. My cerebral palsy makes it harder for me to read because I can't turn the pages of a book. It is hard for me to sound out words due to my speech impediment, so I have to memorize every word. I struggle with reading comprehension sometimes. I am the only one in my classroom with cerebral palsy.

Because of my cerebral palsy, I cannot talk so that people can understand me. Cerebral palsy affects all my muscles, and my tongue is a muscle. My parents and family can understand me most of the time, but other people can't. Sometimes my family has a hard time with things I am saying. So I use my iPad to write out what I want to say. Sometimes this takes a long time, and I get so frustrated.

When I FaceTime and they can't understand what I am saying, we hang up, and then I text what I was trying to say. I don't like it when people are not able to understand me. I know what I am saying, but it is hard for others to know what I am saying. Sometimes I just don't want to talk to people because I know they will not be able to understand me anyway. But one of my favorite things to do is to sit down and talk to people. It is something I have to work hard at and be very patient with all the time. People won't know me if I don't talk and share my story with them. That's why I wrote this book.

SH: Listening to Kaylee share what her life is like with cerebral palsy always causes me to just be silent. It is difficult for me to even know how to respond at times. This is the world she has always known. She experiences things differently, yet all her experiences are what make her unique. Take, for example, the writing of this book, her story. This has been a process of years in the making for her. Imagine taking all afternoon to talk about what you want to say. Then to take the time to type each individual letter on a computer, at times hitting the wrong key over and over and having to start over again and again. Yet she will not give up. She wants to share her story. She wants to be heard. We spent several days in coffee shops transcribing and listening. Watching her insistence on typing and her diligence to accomplish her goal of telling her story was so inspiring to me.

All of our lives are unique. They are uniquely ours. We know what we have experienced, and we understand based on those experiences. We each have a story to tell, and we should tell it. Kaylee did not get to choose her story. You can't choose your story either. But you can choose to share it. Look at all the different stories in the Bible. What did God accomplish through those stories? Think about what you have gained from those stories. Jesus told stories all throughout the Gospels. He was the Master Storyteller.

I find it so encouraging that a young girl with cerebral palsy is so eager to tell her story. She has worked very hard to let others know about her life and who Jesus is to her. She knows that she is the one who can most adequately describe her hard days and her victories. Telling her story means more to Kaylee than just words on the page and a book in hand. It means she has a voice. It means she is not a mistake. She has purpose. She has value. She knows her story has value because of Christ. Your story does too.

In this technology-driven age where we are content to just have social friends and send two-sentence texts, we have lost the beautiful uniqueness of sitting down and sharing face-to-face from the heart. We have become a people who love being popular yet alone. I have had some of my most memorable, life-giving times sitting down with a friend over coffee or lunch and listening to their stories. Their stories inspire me and challenge me. Their stories open up opportunities for prayer and discipleship. Giving someone the opportunity to share their story benefits them and you.

It may not be easy to share your story. It may be uncomfortable at first. You may have a fear of being misunderstood. Maybe you think you are too broken and feel you have to have everything in place before you can share your story. Don't let fear keep you from telling your story. Kaylee certainly has obstacles that have tried to constrain her from telling her story. Yet she chose to use her obstacles as part of her story. She knows she is not the author of her story. She knows God is writing her story, and He is planning the events, the triumphs, the struggles, and all the characters who come into play. You are not the author of your story either. God planned your story long before you knew you had one. Your story matters.

When you choose to share your story, you impact another life for the kingdom of God. As you share who you are, the good and beautiful parts, along with the bad and the ugly, tell how God has worked and is working in your life and how He has redeemed you. Ask God to help you see and take opportunities He provides to share your story.

Thus says the Lord: "Let not the wise man boast in his wisdom, let not the mighty man boast in his might, let not the rich man boast in his riches, but let him who boasts boast in this, that he understands and knows me, that I am the Lord who practices steadfast love, justice, and righteousness in the earth. For in these things I delight, declares the Lord." (Jeremiah 9:23–34)

But for me it is good to be near God; I have made the Lord God my refuge, that I may tell of all your works. (Psalm 73:28)

My mouth will tell of your righteous acts, of your deeds of salvation all the day, for their number is past my knowledge. With the mighty deeds of the Lord God I will come; I will remind them of your righteousness, yours alone. (Psalm 71:15–16)

Oh give thanks to the Lord, for he is good; for his steadfast love endures forever! (Psalm 118:1)

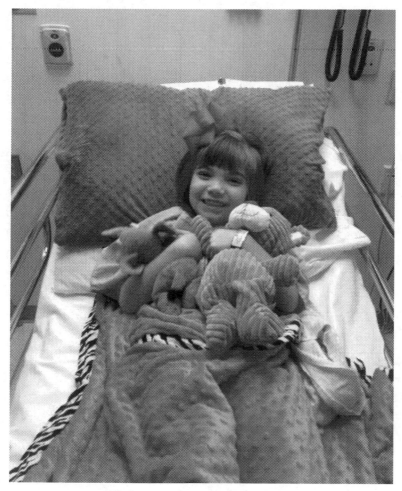

Kaylee in bed with pink blanket
February 2013, Botox procedure

CHAPTER 8

SOMETIMES LIFE IS HARD

It is hard for me to be sick. Having cerebral palsy makes everything harder. Even if I have a cold, it is hard for me. It takes me a lot longer to get over a cold than most people. I get dehydrated easily.

If I get a stomachache, it is really bad too. I get headaches a lot. I take medicine for them, but they still take a long time to go away. Sometimes I have a headache all day long. Any virus can make me a lot sicker, and it takes me much longer to get better. I need my parents to help me when I am sick. I am so thankful that they are always there to help me. Even when they are sick, they have to take care of me.

I first started having seizures when I was a baby. My eyes would not focus, and my lips and eyes would twitch. My parents told me that music would usually help me come out of the seizure. I had an EEG on my brain, but I didn't get much of an explanation.

Once I was rushed to the hospital when I had a seizure. They gave me medicine. I think I was in the hospital two times for different seizures.

My parents always have to monitor me to make sure I don't get too hot. My body doesn't regulate temperature well. If I get too hot, I can have a seizure or become lethargic. Any trip or event that I go to, I have to bring lots of stuff to help me, like cooling cloths, fans, and extra water. I am thankful I haven't had a seizure in a long time.

In February 2013, when I was eight, I had my first Botox treatment at Children's Egleston Hospital in Atlanta.

When I was nine, I had surgery on both of my legs at Children's Hospital of Atlanta, in November 2015. This surgery was to lengthen my tendons in my legs and ankles. I was scared before the surgery because I didn't know what was going to happen. I get anxiety sometimes. My parents prayed with me, and I believed that God would be with me in my surgery. When I woke up, both of my legs were in a cast. It hurt so, so bad. I had to be in the cast for six weeks.

Once I left the hospital and went home, I stayed in my mom and dad's bedroom in their big king-size bed. I had lots of visitors. They came and played games with me while I was in bed. They brought me gifts and talked and prayed with me. I will always remember having friends come over to see me and sit with me. When I was in the casts, I couldn't take a bath, so my mom gave me a bath in bed.

I remember hurting a lot and wanting to get out of the bed, but I couldn't, and I had to learn to be patient and kind to people who were trying to help me during this time. My parents couldn't leave me alone, so they stayed with me or arranged for someone to come sit with me if they had to leave the house. My friends from church would come over and visit with me, and they all signed their names on my casts. My casts were neon pink, and I liked that. I am so glad that I had family and friends who cared about me.

I was sad and bored being in the bed all day for six weeks. It seemed so long. I watched some TV but not much, but my family and friends spent time with me, and that helped. I was happy when I was finally able to get out of the bed and into my wheelchair. This was a difficult time for me, my parents, and grandparents. We did not like or want what was happening. But we believed God knew what He was doing and that He loved us.

I didn't know that God was using this experience to help me in the future. Later on, I had another procedure in the hospital, and it was even more difficult than this one. I was learning to be brave and patient little by little.

I also have a hard time with anxiety. I feel anxious about a lot of different things at different times. I like to know all that is happening to me and what is coming up. Just having cerebral palsy makes me anxious. Being around others and not being able to have them understand me makes me anxious. I am trying to deal with my anxiety. I talk to Jesus about this. He helps me, and my parents do too.

In 2020, I went to see a doctor because I was having stomach problems.

I had acid reflux and swallowing problems. When I drink, a lot of times the liquid comes up and out through my nose. I feel embarrassed by this. I cough, and then food and drink can come out of my mouth. Then someone has to wipe my face. I wish that did not happen.

My parents took me back to the doctor, and they did some tests on me. One doctor told my parents that they were shocked that I had not aspirated already. I didn't know what aspirated meant, but my parents told me that it is when you get food or fluid into your lungs. They felt it was dangerous for me and that I could easily swallow food and liquids into my lungs. They also said I may have to be put on a feeding tube. This made me sad because I love to eat. I knew this worried my mom and dad. They are always trying to decide what is best for me. These are the things I think about at night when I can't sleep.

I had an endoscopy in January 2021. Sometimes I have problems with swallowing and can choke. It has gotten worse over the last year. My parents took me to see a specialist to see what was wrong and what could be done to help me. I know that my cerebral palsy makes it difficult for me to swallow right, but they wanted to make sure it wasn't something more.

First, I had a swallow test. I ate some applesauce, and the doctor watched how I swallowed and how it moved into my stomach. The doctor told my parents that when I swallowed, it was going into my trachea and that I was in danger of asphyxiation. So, they ordered another test to see how my esophagus looked. I couldn't eat or drink anything the day of the test. We drove to Atlanta for the test. I was really anxious about it. What bothered me the most was thinking about having to leave my parents and go into another room without them. I felt like if I needed something, they would not be there for me to tell them. Most people cannot understand me, and this makes me anxious.

I listened to worship music while I waited for the test. This helped me to be calm. I also talked to my dad and mom. I called Manga and talked to her too. I know lots of people were praying for me, and I was happy about that. The test was only about thirty minutes long.

When I woke up, I was still very sleepy. My parents were with me. My throat was sore, and my tongue had blood on it. I was happy that it was over. The doctor said my esophagus looked fine, and my stomach did too. They took a biopsy to check everything out. I learned something from this time. I learned that God can give me strength if I ask Him. I learned how to be brave even when I am afraid. When I have anxiety, I ask God to help me, and He does.

On March 15, 2021, I went into the hospital to have surgery and to have a PEG tube put in. It is a feeding tube, but I will use it mostly for liquids. My parents tell me that they hope the feeding tube will help to get rid of my migraines and the danger of aspirating. The surgery lasted about an hour.

My mom said that the doctor told her that I should've had a feeding tube at six months old. He said that they were great parents because they have taken such great care of me and helped me learn to swallow, eat, and drink.

The surgery went well, but the pain after it was rough. The doctor gave me pain meds and antibiotics through my IV. I was able to eat a little bit in the morning.

A nurse came into the room to teach Mom and Dad how to use the tube, how to clean it and care for me.

The next day, Dad and I went to the chapel at the hospital. He played the piano, and we sang "Amazing Grace" together. I was going home the following day. I was so glad. I had been nervous about getting a tube put in, but I was glad it was over. God helped me again.

My grandparents all came over and visited me after I got home from the hospital. Dad showed them how my GI tube and pump work. I haven't had any headaches since the tube was put in. I am real happy about that.

Later in the week, I was told that I couldn't go back to school for a while now that I had this Gtube. This made me very sad. I guess the teachers were worried about taking care of me. I'm hoping my parents can get it all worked out. I was looking forward to going back to school and seeing my friends and teachers.

I didn't know at the time, but God knew I would need this feeding tube coming up. I would need it not only for liquids but also for food. I'm glad my parents made the right decision for me to have one.

SH: Listening to my young granddaughter tell me about her sickness and suffering left me with mixed feelings. I felt a mixture of sadness and helplessness. But there was another emotion that surfaced as she described her battle with cerebral palsy that I didn't expect. While Kaylee described her sicknesses, surgeries, and the day-to-day suffering she encounters, she did so with a sense of joy that she was an overcomer and that she could continue to overcome. I knew this was God's gift to her. He had shown Himself strong, and she was learning He could be trusted to be faithful in every situation of her life. This is a lesson that few her age even ponder, much less grasp. So, along with the feelings of sadness and helplessness, I saw hope and victory as she shared her story.

Suffering is inescapable in this life. It finds us all and is never welcomed. There is always someone who is suffering more than you and also others who seem to rarely suffer. Yet we all suffer in varied degrees and at varied times throughout our lives.

For the believer, suffering hurts, and its pains are felt no different than for the unbeliever. The loss of a child, the pain of cancer, divorce, disease, natural disasters, disability, poverty, and loneliness all cause great suffering. As believers, we are not immune to suffering. We live in an imperfect world. We have sinful natures. Sorrow and suffering are part of life and seem cruel and at times meaningless.

But for the believer, suffering is not simply dark, meaningless, and cruel. There is purpose in our suffering and a goodness as well. Goodness and suffering, two words that we dare not use in the same sentence. Sometimes we wonder where God is in the middle of our suffering. We feel alone and afraid. Suffering plunges us into the lap of God. It is during those times when we cry out to Him that our faith is built, for He will never forsake us. Joni Eareckson Tada says, "I have suffered, yes. But I wouldn't trade places with anybody in this world to be this close to Jesus."

You will never know the full love of God until you have suffered. How can you experience the comfort of Christ if you have never suffered? It is during those times of suffering when you go to Him that you feel His compassionate hands, hear His words of comfort, and understand that you are totally dependent upon Him. It is during times of suffering that you discover He can be trusted. It is during those times you realize He is good. He alone can bring comfort, calm fears, give you strength to endure, and provide hope. Being dependent upon God is always better than being self-sufficient. Charles Spurgeon said, "I have learned to kiss the wave that throws me against the Rock of Ages."

There is purpose behind your suffering. God uses your suffering in ways that you cannot see. He uses your suffering to bring you closer to Him. He will show you how good He is and how He can be trusted even in the middle of deep hurt and pain. He uses your suffering to bring others to know Him and to trust Him. He comforts you in your suffering so that you can comfort others in their suffering. Christ can be glorified in your suffering. When you realize that, you understand that your suffering is not in vain, and there is even joy within the pain.

Your response to suffering matters. It matters to you and to the world that is watching and listening. Kaylee's response to suffering impacted me. Yes, she hurts. Yes, she is afraid and sad. Yes, she knows there is no cure for cerebral palsy, but she has known the deep love of God and knows He can be trusted. She is finding that she can overcome because He has overcome, and greater is He who is in her than any sickness, sadness, or disability.

> Who shall separate us from the love of Christ? Shall tribulations or distress, or persecution, or famine, or nakedness, or peril, or sword? As it is written: "For Your sake we are killed all day long; We are accounted as sheep for the slaughter." Yet in all these things we are more than conquerors through Him who loved us. For I am persuaded that neither death nor life, nor angels nor principalities nor powers, nor things present nor things to come, nor height nor depth, nor any other created thing, shall be able to separate us from the love of God which is in Christ Jesus our Lord. (Romans 8:35–39)

> For our light and momentary troubles are achieving for us an eternal glory that far outweighs them all. (2 Corinthians 4:17)

> Count it all joy, my brothers, when you meet trials of various kinds, for you know that the testing of your faith produces steadfastness. And let steadfastness have its full effect, that you may be perfect and complete, lacking in nothing. (James 1:2–4)

Blessed be the God and Father of our Lord Jesus Christ, the Father of mercies and God of all comfort, who comforts us in all our affliction, so that we may be able to comfort those who are in any affliction, with the comfort with which we ourselves are comforted by God. For as we share abundantly in Christ's sufferings, so through Christ we share abundantly in comfort too. (2 Corinthians 1:3–5)

CHAPTER 9

WHAT HAPPENED?

On May 6, 2021, I went to the hospital to have a Botox treatment to help my muscles. Lots of people with cerebral palsy have had Botox treatments. I had them once before when I was much younger. This was to help my muscles relax, and then I would have therapy to strengthen my muscles. I was put to sleep and given Botox in my fingers, wrists, thighs, abductors, and toes. I told my mom, "I can't wait to be able to open my hand!"

I am usually very anxious when I have to be put to sleep, but this time I was able to calm myself without the nurse giving me extra medicine. I told my mom that I was fine and that she didn't need to walk me down the hall for my procedure. I learned that God would give me strength and keep me calm, and He did.

After the Botox, when I came home from the hospital, I was able to open my hand really well. I could run my fingers through my hair for the first time. I could also use my legs to walk (with help) much better. My legs would cross over when I tried to walk before, but with the Botox treatment, I could take steps, and my legs did not cross over each other. This helps my parents whenever they take me to the bathroom because it is much easier for me to walk with their help. Plus, I could straighten out my fingers. I could lift my arms straight up high. Praise the Lord! I was very excited about these improvements, and it made me happy that I had gone into the hospital to get the treatments. I did not know what was coming. It is good that I didn't. But I was learning to put my trust in God more and more.

About ten days later, everything changed for me. On Saturday, May 15, my brother, Eli, saved my life. I remember being in my bed that morning and being really sleepy, and I thought that was weird because it was morning time. I started coughing. Mom was in the bathroom, and Daddy heard me and asked Eli to go check on me. I was on my back and choking, and Eli came into my room and saw me. He knew this choking was different. He got my dad and mom to come help me. Dad got me up, and he was worried about me, and I knew something was different. Dad laid me on the couch so he could watch me.

A little later, Pop came over to see me. After Pop left, I started choking really bad. Mom and Dad were both worried about me. I was having a really hard time breathing. It was also hard for me to even hold my head up. I felt so weak and tired. My parents called Nonnie and Poppy to come over and get Eli and Madi. Then Mom and Dad took me to the emergency room. I knew this was bad, and I was scared again. I wondered, *What is happening to me now and why?*

SH: Kaylee titled this chapter "What Happened?" That is a question I think we ask often throughout our lives. I remember well listening to Kaylee talk about having her Botox procedure. She described how she sat down with her parents and her doctor as he explained exactly what the procedure would entail. She was anxious about having it done but was looking forward to it helping her muscles, and she also wanted to be brave. We were all proud of her bravery. She was able to conquer her fears that led up to the procedure, and she knew that God was teaching her how to be strong and to depend on Him.

Once home, she began to see improvements in her body that made her so happy and full of hope. She could raise her arms like never before. She could open her fingers up. She was able to touch the top of her head and rub her fingers through her hair. She showed me how she could take steps as her daddy held her up and how her feet were doing what she wanted them to do. All these things we take for granted, yet she was feeling them for the first time in her life. She was excited, happy, confident, and hopeful.

Then, without warning one Saturday morning, her enthusiasm waned. She was confused, scared, choking, and unable to breathe. Her mind was filled with questions, I'm sure. Questions filled all our minds as we wondered, *Why is this happening? What is God doing?*

Because of COVID, none of the family except Kaylee's parents, Josh and Beth, were allowed to go to the hospital. We were tied to our phones and waited for updates. We could see from pictures and videos how difficult it was for Kaylee. It was beyond what I felt could be endured at the time. How can you no longer be able to swallow your own spit? Who even thinks about swallowing their own spit? Watching her choke, legs flailing, eyes fixed in fear while doctors and nurses suctioned her airway, and seeing her parents hovering over her to calm her and help was just agonizing!

This went on for what seemed like forever. We weren't in the room with her all day or all night, only her parents. Josh and Bethany bore the whole heavy burden of pain and helplessness. Watching them suffer alongside Kaylee and not being able to help either of them only added to the pain.

After weeks of Kaylee being in the hospital, I remember breaking down and coming to the end of holding it all together. I managed to make it through the day, barely … and that evening, in the middle of the night, I knew I had to ask God some things and try to find some answers. So, I got out of bed, grabbed my Bible, some tissues, and a blanket, and headed to the spare bedroom to talk to God.

I have learned over the years that when I feel anxious and overwhelmed about what I don't understand, I should and need to praise God for who I know Him to be. And that's how I began my time with the Lord. As I praised Him for who He is and who He has been, I knew He was listening to me. I knew He would not be scared or shocked by my feelings. He already knew what I was thinking and feeling. So, I shared with Him all my fears, frustrations, and questions.

I had questions, and I asked them. "What's the point of having a child with a disability receive some form of help only to have that help make it even worse for her later? Why did You even allow this to happen? Couldn't You have just kept this from her? How much can her parents bear?"

I would ask a question and sob. Read a verse of scripture and sob. Sit quietly and sob. Alone in the quiet but not alone at all. I could feel the presence of Christ. I knew He was right there with me. Back and forth— questions, crying, scripture, and praise.

It was the Word that brought me peace. It was His very own words. When I surrendered to His Word, my soul was quieted. I surrendered my anxieties, my worries, and even my questions to Him. His Word assured me that in all my questions, all my lack of understanding, He was not forsaking me, Kaylee, or her parents. I read several passages that night. I intentionally looked up verses telling me who God was. In the crucial, tough places of your life, you really need to know who God is.

I read the verse in Isaiah 46:9–10 that says, "Remember the former things of old; for I am God, and there is no other; I am God, and there is none like me, declaring the end from the beginning and from ancient times things not yet done, saying, 'My counsel shall stand, and I will accomplish all my purpose.'" This reminded me that God is all-knowing. I can trust that He knows everything we're going through today and everything we will go through tomorrow. He can be trusted. He wasn't surprised by the events taking place. He was in control.

I read the verse in Romans 11:33 that says, "Oh, the depth of the riches and wisdom and knowledge of God! How unsearchable are His judgments and how inscrutable His ways!" This reassured me that God is wise. He knows what He is doing in the life of Kaylee and in the lives of all of us. He sees everything in perfect clarity and is working toward perfection. He is always doing the wisest thing in our lives. He really is working all things out in the best possible way, even when we don't see it or feel it.

I read the verse in Deuteronomy 7:9 that says, "Know therefore that the Lord your God is God, the faithful God, who keeps covenant and steadfast love with those who love him and keep his commandments, to a thousand generations" This one I read out loud! I proclaimed, "This means I can count on You to be good, loving and gracious. During all our times of pain, suffering, questions, fear … God, you are faithful."

I left my time with God that evening different from when I came. Kaylee was still not well. I had no idea if or when she would get better. My heart still ached for her parents. Most, if not all, of my questions were still unanswered. Nevertheless, I went to bed knowing that God heard my prayer, that He is trustworthy, full of wisdom, faithful, and good. I could trust Him with this situation, and He had everything under control. God will use this situation for His glory and for the good of His people. He will work all things out for our good, and He will give us all the grace we need to endure it.

It's OK to ask, "What happened?" All throughout our lives, we will have questions, especially during tragedies and suffering. Go to God in your suffering. God can handle your lamentations and your questions. Bring your praise as well. Allow Him to speak to you from His Word. Trust in the one who is wise, faithful, loving, and good. He will answer your questions—not in the way you think you need but in a way that shows you who He is. In turn, He may ask you some questions. "Will you trust Me? Am I good?"

> "Then you will call upon me and come and pray to me, and I will hear you. You will seek me and find me, when you seek me with your heart." (Jeremiah 29:12–13)

> The Lord is near to the broken-hearted and saves the crushed in spirit. (Psalm 34:18)

Kaylee in hospital bed May 2021

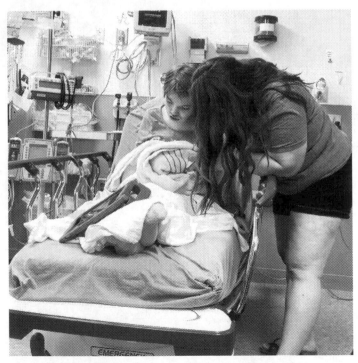

Kaylee with Mom in hospital bed May 2021

Chapter 10

At the Hospital, Day by Day

I don't remember all that happened to me during this time, but I remember some things. I will tell you what I remember on certain days. On May 15, when I was at the hospital, the doctors began to know what was happening to me. The doctor told my parents that I had been given too much Botox. It messed up my whole body. It caused me to be unable to swallow. I felt like I was choking even when I just tried to breathe. I choked on my own spit, which made it so hard for me to breathe.

Mom told me that the Botox had affected my whole body. The places on my body that were already bad and weak from cerebral palsy were now even worse. I did not understand all of this. It was so confusing to me.

The doctors decided to try to reverse the Botox, but they had never tried to do that before. I was put in the intensive care part of the hospital. I was very weak and couldn't even hold my head up because my muscles had too much Botox in them. I felt like I did when I would wake up from surgery, very sleepy. My head was hard to hold up, and my neck felt heavy. I could not really lie all the way down because I would start to choke. I felt very scared about what was happening to me. I could tell my mom and dad were very worried about me.

On May 16, I was finally able to get back in my power wheelchair. I had help holding my head up in the chair. My occupational therapist and I went to see the therapy dog. I had never felt a dog with my hand before. I wish I had a dog. Maybe my parents will get me one. That night was better than the night before, and I was able to sleep.

A few days later, my little brother, Eli, graduated from kindergarten. I wish I could have seen him graduate, but I couldn't leave the hospital. My parents went, and Pop and Manga were given permission to come stay with me at the hospital till they got back. I was glad to see Manga and Pop. We had a good time talking.

I had one bad episode of choking while they were with me. Manga had to call the nurse to come suction me. I wish that wouldn't have happened. They left, and I didn't see them again for a long time.

On the nineteenth, Dad and I went to the hospital garden and sat outside. We sang some worship songs. I was tired and weak but was glad to be outside and singing. Once I went to bed, I slept most of the night. It was better than the other nights.

But the next morning, I got nauseated and started choking. My dad used the suction machine and suctioned me out. I was moving my legs in the bed and trying so hard to breathe. I just couldn't get any air. It is scary to not be able to breathe. I was afraid.

I had a swallow study. I was given eggs, and they didn't go down. Next, I tried grits. They went down a little bit better. These were very, very tiny bites. It took a lot of swallows to get them down. I ended up needing suctioning. I just couldn't really swallow anything. This made me sad.

One part of the day was good. I had a therapy dog come see me. His name was Olaf. I loved it.

A few days later, I had a rough night. It was so bad. I choked a lot and had to be suctioned a lot. The medicine the doctors were giving me to stop the Botox was causing my shoulders, hips, and knees to hurt. My parents told me it was tightening my joints. My mom was going to tell them to bring the dose down so that I didn't have that kind of pain.

Also, when I got my feeding through my Gtube, it was coming back up in my throat. That made me choke even more and feel horrible.

My parents took turns staying with me at night at the hospital. One night, dad stayed, and then the other night, mom stayed. They drove back and forth from home to the hospital. I knew they were tired, but I was glad that they were taking turns staying with me.

It had been seventeen days since I'd had my Botox injections. It had been ten days since I had eaten anything. I had been in the hospital for nine days. I missed tasting food. I had learned to appreciate the taste of food.

I had a hard time getting comfortable before bedtime. My dad stayed with me that night. He sang to me a song that he wrote and played his guitar. Hearing the song made me feel peaceful. I remember hearing the words, "We Know Our God Hears." I knew there were lots of people praying for me and my family. And I knew God heard their prayers. I believed that God heard me and all the prayers.

A few days later, I had a busy day. I had three therapy sessions. In physical therapy, they worked on helping me hold my body and neck up and also having more control when I was sitting up. In speech therapy, the therapist worked with me to help my swallowing. Mom said it was like sit-ups for my neck muscles. In occupation therapy, I was given toys to squeeze and grab to help with my hands. I used some Play-Doh too. All my muscles are weak. I need lots of therapy. It's like starting back over.

On May 26, my dad changed my Gtube. The nurses showed him how, and he did it. My parents told me that they had decided to transfer me to Scottish Rite Inpatient Rehab. So they took me by ambulance to rehab, and my mom rode with me.

I had another rough time at bedtime. When Mom was helping me get comfortable in the bed, I started choking. Then I started vomiting. I kept doing this over and over. I was so scared and so weak. I wanted it to stop. My throat felt raw. Nurses had to suction deep down to my esophagus to help me. I could tell my mom was scared too. We both were.

A few days later, I had my first full day of therapy. I had physical and recreational therapy once and then speech and occupation therapy twice.

I had a therapy dog come and visit me in my room. I let him climb up in the bed with me. He was so gentle and calm. I liked that. After all the therapy and the visit with the dog, I had to take a long nap because I was so tired. I ended up having a migraine the rest of the day and vomited.

May 29

I can't have visitors in the hospital. But today Pop and Eli stopped by Scottish Rite, and they were able to see me and Dad through the gate of the garden. My Nonnie and Poppy came one day too, and we visited at the gate. I have missed my brother, Eli, and my little sister, Madi, so much. I FaceTime them as much as I can just to see them. I even miss hearing them arguing and running around. Madi and Eli have been staying at my grandparents' houses and with others in our family. They have been having fun. I will be so glad to see them.

May 31

The chaplain at Scottish Rite found out my dad was a pastor and asked him to lead the worship service at the chapel today. I love hearing my dad sing. It helps both of us. I think it helps others in the hospital too.

I had a really rough day and night. Lots of choking even though they gave me more medicine. There were four times in the night that I had to have deep suctioning. It is so scary for me. I feel like I'm suffocating. My feeding tube came out too. It was so painful when they put another one in. They had to hold me down to do it. The doctor decided I need a bigger Gtube. I am glad my dad was with me. He calms me down, and I know I am safe with him.

June 4

I had more energy today and was able to do six therapy sessions. I am working hard to get strong and hope to get back to the way I was before. I hardly ever took naps before all this happened unless I was sick. Now I seem to be tired all the time.

June 5

I decorated my hospital room today with some art that I made during therapy. It is a picture of a llama. We also put some pictures from Eli and Madi up on my wall. I had three therapy sessions today. I decided to make an Amazon wish list because so many people are asking what I would like. They want to send me gifts. It made me happy to know that others were thinking of me.

I started wearing wrist splints and learning a new way to use my iPad. Since all this happened with the Botox, I haven't been able to text and use my iPad like I used to. All my fingers are out straight now. They get in the way, and I touch all the keys at one time. It is so frustrating to me because this is how I talked to people, by texting them. Everything is different now.

I get lots of medicines through my Gtube now. I think it is like ten medicines I get every day. I used to only get a medicine if I had a headache. Or my mom would use essential oils to help me. I have to keep taking all this medicine until the Botox is gone from my body. The doctors say it will probably take three to four months, but they don't know for sure.

June 6

At the hospital today while I was in rehab, they made me some solid AFOs to strengthen my ability to bear weight. They are the most comfortable that I have ever worn. AFOs are ankle foot orthosis. They are like braces to help with movement in my lower legs, ankles, and feet. They support my weak muscles. They help me keep my feet and ankles in a normal position.

I have spent twenty-four days in the hospital. It seems so long. I miss my home, my brother and sister, my grandparents, and all my cousins, aunts, and uncles. I miss going to church and seeing all my friends. I listen to worship music every day, and I am able to watch my church service every Sunday on my iPad, but it is not the same as being there. I want to be there.

SH: As Kaylee recalled her time at the hospital and described what she remembered day by day, I thought about the goodness of God. Even though each day was full of uncertainty, pain, and fear, God's goodness was inescapable.

Kaylee saw and felt God's goodness in the faces and in the touch and love of her parents. God's goodness was evident to her in the care of the nurses and doctors. She felt the goodness of God in the fresh air of the garden as she sang with her dad. The gentleness of the therapy dog and the calm that he brought to her was also the goodness of God. Friends and family asking her to make a wish list, yes … the goodness of God. Therapists taking extra time and interest, all the goodness of God. In her day-to-day telling, God's goodness spoke too.

I have always loved to journal. What started out as a little girl keeping a diary turned into a lifetime of journaling. At first, it was just to write down my thoughts. It has evolved over the years to contain scripture, prayers, blessings, and all things personal. I find that writing down the happenings of my day causes me to see beyond the ink. I can see God at work. At times, I can even see my sin as I write down my thoughts and struggles. Journaling helps me to slow down and process my thoughts. It helps me to put my feelings to words. It gives me the opportunity to record some of the blessings of God in my life. Journaling causes me to reflect on my spiritual growth or lack of spiritual growth. Journaling gives me the space to write out my prayers and meditate on scripture. It helps me to see the goodness of God throughout all the seasons of my life.

When we are in the middle of suffering, it is so easy to focus on the pain. Pain demands our attention and a response. It brings with it fear, worry, and disappointment. It can consume our bodies and our thought life. There is a refining that comes with pain. I think this refining comes because it takes us to a place where all we can see is our lack and God's grace. It is in those times, if we look, we can see, touch, and even taste the goodness of God. Charles Spurgeon said, "Remember the goodness of God in the frost of adversity."

When you cannot be comforted by others, when your body groans and no aid can be given, when loneliness is your closest friend, when the doctors offer no remedy or answer … look. Search for the goodness of God. It is all around you. There are endless ways to see the goodness of God.

Open your eyes to God's goodness that you see in people. The nurse, neighbor, friend, or stranger who offers kindness, help, and care is an extension of God's goodness. A visit from a friend and a phone call to offer encouragement—these are both gifts of God's goodness. The therapists and nurses allowed Kaylee to experience God's goodness on the hardest of days. Family and friends calling to find out how they could send her gifts showed her God's goodness too. Kaylee knew the sacrifices her parents were making. This was God's goodness to her as well.

Open your eyes to God's goodness in nature. There's nothing I enjoy more than seeing God in nature. God's attributes can be seen in the things that He has created. I remember many years ago feeling overwhelmed and alone. Struggling to sleep and find comfort, I climbed out of bed in the middle of the night. As I walked into my living room, I could see light. No light was on inside. There was a beautiful glow flowing in from the outside. I opened my door to find the biggest, brightest, most glorious moon shining above my house. I immediately thought of God and His power, His goodness, and His complete love for me. Seeing the moon in all its splendor made my situation seem small and His power and might seem so vast.

God is constantly reminding me of His faithfulness and goodness in the sunset, in the details of a rose, or watching a bird build a nest. All of creation speaks to the glory of God—the goodness of God as the rain covers the earth, the goodness of God in the discovery of a rainbow. God takes pleasure in His creation, and so should we.

Learn to fully appreciate what God created. He said it is good and it is full of His goodness. Take the time to touch the petal of a flower and notice its intricate detail. Look at the stunning artistry of a butterfly. In doing so, think of God as Creator and sustainer. Use what God has made to remind yourself of His goodness.

Kaylee was able to experience God's goodness as she sat outside in the fresh air of the garden at the hospital and sang with her dad. She was able to find calm and enjoy the softness of the golden retriever's coat when he climbed in bed with her. These were little glimpses of God's goodness in the midst of her day-to-day suffering and hurt.

Open your eyes to God's goodness in His Word. That Bible you have sitting on your shelf has power and value. We are very needy when we are hurting. Pain causes us to listen to fear and can keep us from focusing on the truth that comes from God's Word. We try to comfort ourselves with many things while we are suffering. Some work, at least for a while. God's Word is a proven source of comfort. It gives us hope, peace, and wisdom in times of suffering. It is powerful in that it is able to pierce the heart and provide exactly what we need.

Spending time in God's Word helps to remind us of His love and goodness. John Calvin said, "But a faithful believer will in all circumstances meditate on the mercy and fatherly goodness of God." The song that Kaylee's dad sang to her, "We Know Our God Hears," gave her weary body rest and her fearful heart hope. Listening to her pastor preach the Gospel while she was in the hospital allowed her to hear God's Word, and she was reminded of His comfort and goodness. Kaylee even mentioned how she enjoyed watching her church service but how she wished she could be there in person. I think she understands something about the goodness of God that we many times forget. She enjoys celebrating God's goodness with His people.

Those are just a few ways to look for God's goodness. It is an inexhaustible list. A.W. Tozer says, "The goodness of God is infinitely more wonderful than we will ever be able to comprehend." Our minds and eyes can never grasp all the ways that God is good. But it surely doesn't hurt to try. In fact, it definitely helps. I encourage you, as you walk through suffering and pain, try writing it down. Recall the day-to-day. Look for the goodness of God in people, in nature, and in His Word. Write down all the ways you see and feel His goodness. As the words come and the ink hits the paper, you will see how God's goodness manifests itself in your life. Right in the middle of your pain, wherever you may be, God's goodness is all around. Look and see!

> The Lord is good to all, and his mercy is over all that he has made. (Psalm 145:9)

> Oh, taste and see that the Lord is good! Blessed is the man who takes refuge in Him. (Psalm 34:8)

> O give thanks to the Lord, for He is good; for His steadfast love endures forever! (1 Chronicles 16:34)

> I am the good shepherd. The good shepherd lays down his life for the sheep. (John 10:11)

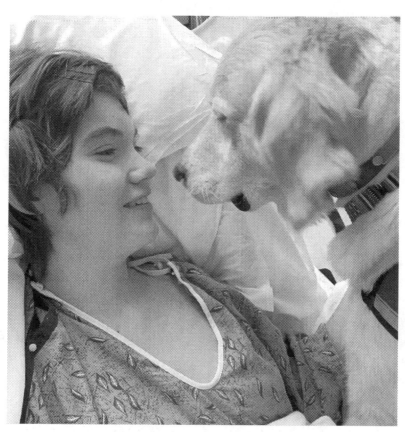

Kaylee with therapy dog in hospital

Chapter 11

It's So Good to Be Home

Finally, on June 7, I went home! When we drove up our driveway, my brother, sister, grandparents, and cousins were in the yard with posters that said, "Welcome Home, Kaylee." Madi saw our car and threw her poster down and ran to the car. When I saw Madi, I started crying so loud. I was happy to see her and hug her and Eli. I love being home! When I went inside, I saw the painting I made for my parents a long time ago. It hangs on the wall in my room and says, "It's so good to be home."

I was so happy to be home. I wasn't in my own bed, but I was in a hospital bed in my own room. It was so good to see Eli and Madi. Even when they both got in trouble, I was glad to hear it. Dad and Mom took turns sleeping in my room. They had a mattress on the floor, and I had my hospital bed. Mom had all the medicine to take care of me and the suction machine if we needed it. They both knew how to use it. They had used it with me lots of times at the hospital.

I couldn't see a lot of people during this time. I had to be careful not to catch a cold or get sick, since I was not able to swallow right. I missed going out and doing the things I could do. My parents had to stay with me all the time. I know they missed going out too.

My grandparents came to see me some, and I liked that. I missed being able to eat with my family. I missed eating so much. That was one of my favorite things to do. My family ate at the table, and I sat in my recliner and got food from the Gtube. I usually called Manga and talked to her while they were eating.

One day, my teacher, Ms. Bolton, came to see me. She helped me, and even Eli and Madi, paint. I loved my visit with her.

June 26 was the first day I had been out of the house in forty-four days, not counting the time in the hospital. I went to Target with my family. I was really nervous before we left. My mom made sure to bring all the suction equipment just in case we needed it, but we didn't, and I was so glad. I was tired after just going to Target though.

My parents worked with me to practice my swallowing once a day to keep my throat used to it. I practiced with drinking a Yoo-hoo because it was thin. It took me lots of swallows to get just a little bit down, but it tasted so good on my tongue after not having anything for so long.

I received lots of gifts when I was in the hospital and when I came home from the hospital. It seemed like every day I would get several packages to open. Some of the things that were given to me were cameras, games, sheets, hoodies, T-shirts, an umbrella for my wheelchair, a massager, blankets, sound machine, lights for my wheelchair tires, theraputty ... so much stuff.

People also sent me cards and text messages. They brought lots of meals for my family and also bought groceries. A friend also built a table and used it as a fundraiser for me and my family. People came and cut our grass and worked in our yard to help too. All of this made me know that people love us and want to help us. I know this is God showing His love to me.

My mom and dad finally got to go out to dinner for the first time by themselves in a long, long, time. Pop and Manga watched Eli and Madi. A friend came to stay and take care of me. Her name is Emily. She is a paramedic, so I knew she would know how to take care of me, especially if I started choking. I was glad my parents were able to leave me, like they used to, but I was still nervous. But I was able to do it, even if I was afraid. I didn't have a choking episode, so that was good.

I started having therapy at home. Some days I had three therapy sessions in one day. I was so tired after I was finished. I usually went to bed. When I got really tired, that was when it was hard for me to swallow. I was working to get strong again. All my muscles seemed so weak. It was like starting all over again.

July 4 was my first time back to church in a long, long time. I was so excited to go to church, but I was a little worried that I might start choking.

When I went into the church, I could hear everyone singing. My dad was singing my favorite song, "Every Victory." My mom started crying. I loved hearing that song, and I loved being in church again.

But after a while, maybe fifteen minutes, I got really weak. So I asked my mom to take me home. I did the best I could. I wished I could have stayed, but I just couldn't. I felt better when I got back home.

SH: There's no place like home. Our homes are places we live, laugh, love, and serve one another. It is the place where we feel accepted and cared for. Home is not found in the size or value of your house. Home is not simply made comfortable by the contents within. Home is a place where you feel you belong and those whom you live with share your values and beliefs. Home can only be what it is meant to be when Christ is the head. You've heard the saying, "Christ is the head of this house, the unseen guest at every meal, the silent listener to every conversation." His presence is what makes for a truly beautiful, peaceful home.

When parents live under the authority of Christ and His Word, they find all they need to create a loving home. Kaylee knows the value of a loving home. God has blessed her with godly parents who strive to obey Him and to teach and train their children well. Kaylee yearned to be home after such a long hospital stay. She knew she would be comfortable, safe, and well taken care of. At home, she has been the recipient of countless hours of service. She has seen her family extend grace to her over and over again. She has felt forgiveness, encouragement, and correction. This is where she wished to be.

Creating a home that provides love, protection, and enjoyment to our families doesn't just magically appear once you are married or once that first child arrives. Signing mortgage papers isn't a guarantee that you'll have a home. Maybe a house but not a home. The challenges to creating a godly home are real and require intentional work on your part, lots of prayer, and obedience to the voice of God.

There are tons of things that contend for God's place in our hearts when it comes to creating a godly home. Convenience, entertainment, careers, hobbies, and even the self strive to keep us from honoring Christ with our homes. We focus on the here and now and not on the things of eternity. We run to websites and books to find the best method to raise our children and create loving homes; all the while, the best source of wisdom sits untouched on our shelf.

God's Word contains everything you need to create a godly home. Yes, there are numerous voices of godly wisdom that can instruct us, but none greater than the words of God. How about asking the one who created the family how it should work and function?

All our beliefs and values should be based upon the Word of God. Our children need to know the truth that is found in God's Word. You will display that truth to them by reading it and teaching it to them and by living accordingly. You, as parents, are responsible for teaching your children the truths found in God's Word. Don't delegate this responsibility to the school system, the television, or even the church. It is your responsibility.

The day will come, sooner than you think, when your children will be grown and leave your home. All they will take with them is love and truth. The time you invested in buying that bigger house, paying for that pool, making sure they had the coolest in-style clothes, hauling them around to every event that seemed to matter ... won't matter! They will step out the door of your home with two things ... love and truth. Your children will understand the value and worth of those virtues throughout the rest of their lives. Love for the things of God and knowing the truth found in the Word of God are the building blocks of home.

We cannot teach what we do not know. Perhaps that's why we don't. Our children see what's most important to us. Do we value the Word of God? Do our children know what God loves?

You have a certain amount of time to teach those things. Use your time wisely. Pray for your children. Ask God to give you a servant's heart. Be consistent in discipline. Turn off the television, put down your phones, and invest in the lives of your children. They are not concerned with how much money you are making. They could care less if you have one thousand Facebook friends and Instagram followers. They do, however, care and long for your love and the truth of God. If you don't give it to them, who will?

Someone will give them a false love, and someone will fill their innocent minds with lies. Obey the Lord and create a home that honors Him. It will cost you. It won't be easy. You will feel like a failure at times. You will need to make choices that glorify God. You may need to prioritize worship, Bible reading, church attendance, and teaching over other things vying for your time and attention.

But don't give up or get lazy. Spend time with the Lord and let Him show you how to be a godly parent and how to teach and train your children well. His desire is for every child to have a place to call home—a place like Kaylee longed to be. Because on the toughest of days, the days of sorrow and pain, they will want to go home. They will long for a place where love lives and where truth is spoken, and they will be able to say, like Kaylee, "It feels good to be home."

> And these words that I command you today shall be on your heart. You shall teach them diligently to your children, and shall talk of them when you sit in your house, and when you walk by the way, and when you lie down, and when you rise. You shall bind them as a sign on your hand, and they shall be as frontlets between your eyes. You shall write them on the door posts of your house and on your gates. (Deuteronomy 6:6–9)

> Husbands, love your wises, as Christ loved the church and gave Himself up for her. (Ephesians 5:25)

> Wives, submit to your own husbands, as to the Lord. For the husband is the head of the wife even as Christ is the head of the church, His body, and is Himself its Savior. Now as the church submits to Christ, so also wives should submit in everything to their husbands. Husband, love your wives, as Christ loved the church and gave Himself up for her, that he might sanctify her, having cleansed her by the washing of water with the word, so that he might present the church to himself in splendor, without spot or wrinkle or any such thing, that she might be holy and without blemish. In the same way husbands should love their wives as their own bodies. He who loves his wife loves himself. For no one ever hated his own flesh, but

nourishes and cherishes it, just as Christ does the church. (Ephesians 5:22–29)

Children, obey your parents in everything, for this pleases the Lord. (Colossians 3:20)

Jesus said to him, "I am the way, and the truth, and the life. No one comes to the Father except through me." (John 14:6)

"This is my commandment, that you love one another, even as I have loved you." (John 15:12)

Finally Home - Family Hug

CHAPTER 12

I CAN

I am working on my swallowing every day. I am able to eat some oatmeal for breakfast and have tried macaroni and cheese. Every day, my parents work with me to get my swallowing back. They know I love to eat, and they want me to be able to do that again.

I also work every day on my muscles and hand movements during therapy. I look forward to every therapy session because I know this is how I will get stronger and get back to how I used to be. I am slowing improving, and we are all happy about that. I haven't had any choking episodes during the night for a while.

I am now in extensive therapy. This is therapy that I go to four days a week for four hours each day. Like I said, it is hard work, but I love doing it. It is what I have to do to get better.

My teacher continues to come to my home and teach me. I miss going to school but am so thankful that she comes to see me. Hopefully, I will be going back to my school this fall.

I have been back to my church, and I am able to stay for the whole service. This makes me so happy. One Sunday after church, my family and I went out for lunch. This was the first time I had been out to eat in a restaurant in a long, long time. I was anxious and nervous about each bite of food, but I did it. I was able to eat some food, and it felt so good to be out with my family. It reminded me of the way things used to be.

I just celebrated my fifteenth birthday with my family. My mom is the best at planning parties. She and I decided on a fiesta theme. She made tacos, chips, and all the toppings. My family was there, and my grandparents too. I was able to eat, and that made me so happy. I am improving every day. I can see that I'm getting better.

I have a goal that I have set for myself. I told this goal to my parents and grandparents. They are encouraging me to meet my goal. My goal is to be able to eat and drink on my own. I hope one day I can have the Gtube taken out and go back to how I used to be. I know this will take time and I will need to do what is best for my body. But I think I can do it!

Sometimes I wonder why all this happened to me. Why did I have to get too much Botox and make my muscles even worse than they already were? Like I said in the first chapter, sometimes I wonder why I was born with cerebral palsy, but I think it is because God made me special and wanted me to show how strong He is. I have to remind myself of this. I can do what I need to do because God is helping me.

SH: This book would be incomplete if I didn't share my heart regarding children with disabilities. There are more than three million children in the United States with a disability. These are the fortunate, in that they were allowed to be born. Statistics show that 67 percent of US pregnancies where it is suggested the baby would be born with Down syndrome end in abortion. In other countries, the abortion rates may be greater than 90 percent. Our world is becoming less and less graced by the souls we label as disabled or special needs.

We live in a world where it is acceptable to ignore those who are not physically or mentally in the norm. In fact, the world is set up in such a way to cause those with disabilities to hide and remain unnoticed and silent. Yes, resources and laws have been implemented to help those with disabilities, but have we as a culture embraced those with special needs as Christ desires us to? Have we, as the church, failed to be a refuge for the disabled? Has the church become just another place that those with special needs should avoid? In the United States, children with disabilities are much more likely to never attend church than children with no disability or special need. Why is this?

There is a tremendous void when all the members of a congregation do not have the opportunity to get to know and benefit from the gifts of people with special needs in their church. Welcoming children with disabilities benefits the children, their families, and the congregation. Ministering to special needs children and their families is a blessing, not a burden. Special needs children are uniquely blessed by God, and it is a privilege to get to know them, learn from them, and see God's grace manifested in them. Children with disabilities encounter many challenges. Church should not be one of them. Kaylee is blessed by a loving church where she is accepted, valued, and loved. There's nothing I enjoy more on a Sunday morning than hearing her sing and worship the Lord.

When you get to know a special needs child, your life will be changed for the better. Yes, it is different. Yes, it may take you out of your comfort zone. But the reward is much greater than any fear you may have or any degree of inconvenience you feel.

When was the last time you encountered a disabled, handicapped, or special needs child? Was it awkward? Did you find yourself looking the other way? Feeling pity but moving past like you never even truly noticed? In one of Kaylee's writings, I was having difficulty understanding her. We were FaceTiming on the phone. So, she used her computer program that speaks aloud what she types. The words were typed with her fingers, spoken by a computer's voice, yet all from her heart. "I want people to understand people with disabilities and take time to know us. I want people to not be afraid to talk to me and listen to me. We may look like our lives do not matter, but our lives do matter."

Needless to say, it was a beautiful moment that we shared together. But I believe this is what all children with special needs long for each of us to hear and understand. They want you to know that their lives matter, and they want you to take the time to know them. Such a simple request, yet we often fail so miserably.

John Piper, in his book *Disability and the Sovereign Goodness of God*, writes, "And I would just plead in passing- children, young people, and adults - see people with disabilities. And I don't mean see them like the priest and the Levite on the Jericho Road, passing by on the other side. This is our natural reflex - see and avoid. But we are not natural people. We are followers of Jesus. We have the Spirit of Jesus in our hearts. We have been seen and touched in all our brokenness by an attentive, merciful Savior."

The beauty and insight that a special needs child possesses are priceless. It is to your benefit and joy to get to know, love, and serve such a soul.

One day, Kaylee and I were together sitting on the back porch. Kaylee has a unique ability to remember the last time she was with you and what you talked about. I had been feeling ill and was having some heart problems that turned out to be acid reflux. I had shared this with her several days prior. On this particular fall day, Kaylee asked me, "Manga, how's your heart?"

I said, "Oh, it's about the same, maybe a little better."

She said, "No, Manga. I mean how's your heart? How's your heart with the Lord?"

I'm thinking physical. She's thinking spiritual.

Her life is always filled with physical challenges. Every day, every moment, she is faced with limitations physically. Trust me, she understands the challenges and sorrows of her physical limitations. Yet she was concerned with the challenges and sorrow of my soul. It is the experience of her physical limitations, her brokenness, that allows her to be extra sensitive to the beauty of the soul. I would have never known the wondrous blessing of understanding these kind of lessons, if not for knowing her. Her value is in her brokenness. She shows me my brokenness.

Being broken is not bad. Brokenness can be embraced. In fact, God welcomes brokenness. God will not despise a broken spirit, and God does not despise a broken body. Jesus's body was broken for us. Our brokenness drives us to Christ. Ministry to the broken, disabled, special needs child is a privilege. Those who the world seems to avoid and reject due to their brokenness, I pray we, as the church, would embrace and welcome.

I love this quote from Michale Beates, "As followers of Christ, we must respect God's creation of all people, and see them not as problems to be ignored or hidden away. Rather, we must see them as mirrors of our own brokenness, and as divine windows through which we can catch glimpses of God's grace. We must do whatever we can to respect God's image in even the most broken and twisted lives. Even the least of these carries intrinsic dignity and worth."

When we take the time to know and value someone with a disability, we create a space for them that they cherish. A disabled child lives in a world that screams, "You can't do this," or "This is no place for you." Certainly, we as the church, as followers of Christ, can scream, "You can do this!" and "There is a place for you!" We should be their biggest supporters, their loudest cheerleaders, their most frequent servers. Yes, you can do it! You have value! You are loved! How can we serve you?

> But he said to me, "My grace is sufficient for you, for My power is made perfect in weakness. Therefore I will boast all the more gladly in my weaknesses, so that the power of Christ may rest on me." (2 Corinthians 12:9)

> And his disciples asked him, "Rabbi, who sinned, this man or his parents, that he was born blind?" Jesus answered, "It was not that this man sinned, or his parents, but that the works of God might be displayed in him." (John 9:2–3)

> He said also to the man who had invited him, "When you give a diner or a banquet, do not invite your friends or your brothers, or you relatives or rich neighbors, lest they also invite you in return and you be repaid. But when you give a feast, invite the poor, the crippled, the lame, the blind, and you will be blessed, because they cannot repay you. For you will be repaid at the resurrection of the just." (Luke 14:12–14)

CHAPTER 13

IT'S ALL RIGHT

One thing I like to say is "It's all right!" I say this because there is no reason to stress out about life because Jesus is in control. I say it all the time. It is a habit for me now. Even in little things that can cause me anxiety, I say, "It's all right!" Then I laugh because it reminds me that I say it a lot, but it also helps me to know that everything is going to be all right.

My life is hard. Most of my days are hard. I am learning how to find hope in Jesus every day with my cerebral palsy. I am young and do not know what will happen next. I know there is no cure for my cerebral palsy. But I know *it is all right*! Ha! I said it again!

My family is learning how to find hope in Jesus, too, because of me. I hope you can also find hope and help from Jesus after reading my story. That is why I wrote it, so that you will not be sad about the hard parts of your life. There is always hope, and God knows what He is doing.

Your story is different. It's not like mine. It is unique too. I would like to hear it. I hope you will share it so it can bring hope to others.

SH: At the very beginning of Kaylee's story, I asked her why she wanted to write this book. Her response, "The reason I am writing this book is so that you will enjoy your life and learn to be happy. I am learning how to be happy by following Jesus's example. I love my life, but at times, it is very hard for me. Even though it is hard, following Jesus helps me to be strong."

We can choose to enjoy our lives, choose to have joy while in deep suffering and loss. Choosing or learning those things does not nullify our suffering or loss. The heart still aches, and the exhaustion and tears do not vanish. Yet experiencing joy and enjoyment in our lives during suffering affirms our trust in God. John Piper says, "Hurting and joy are not opposites; they're not contrary. They can exist at the same time." Our joy is found in God's unfailing love, His sovereignty, and in believing that He is good. Finding Jesus in your suffering is more important than anything else. Finding Christ faithful, loving, and compassionate is of more value than anything we could lose or any amount of suffering in this life.

I wish I had a dollar for every time I've heard Kaylee say, "It's all right!" I find I catch her saying it the most when she is in need of something and you can't help her right at that moment. She looks at you and says, "It's all right." You see, Kaylee is aware of her need. She knows that she is dependent upon others for her care, for eating, for using the bathroom, for mobility ... all her needs. She relies upon the kindness and servitude of others to help her in most all situations.

Kaylee is perhaps the most patient person I know. She has learned at the age of fifteen what patience consists of. We all want to be patient, but none of us like the lessons we have to endure to be granted patience. Kaylee's lessons in patience began at birth. Total dependence has a course of action that almost always produces patience.

Patience is defined as the capacity to accept or tolerate delay, trouble, or suffering without getting angry or upset. It's a beautiful virtue but not easily obtained; nor does it happen instantly. God knows how to cultivate patience in each individual life. He definitely uses trials to perfect our patience. When we allow God to lead us through our trials, and we patiently endure, we see Him at work. Our faith is then made stronger as He works all things out for our good and His glory. Trials are never for nothing, and our pain is never wasted. Obtaining patience has a reward. The reward is stronger faith. Who doesn't want stronger faith?

Having the attitude of "It's all right," as Kaylee said, helps her to know that God is in control and there is no need to stress out! It is not the mindset of "I don't care" but rather "I do care, and I know that God cares more, and He will perfect that which concerns me."

What is important to you is important to your heavenly Father. Cast your cares upon Him. Acknowledge you are needy. Ask Jesus to make you aware of His nearness. Take time to rest in His goodness. Allow Him to carry you in those times of deep suffering, pain, and disappointment. In order to do that, you have to relinquish control. You have to surrender your fears. You have to trust that God is good. You have to allow patience to do its work within you. You have to choose joy. It is then that you can say with great calm and resolve, "It's all right." It is then that you can truly live and enjoy your life, regardless of the pain and suffering, and still experience joy. Your walk will be unique. It will be uniquely yours as Christ leads the way.

> Be still before the Lord and wait patiently for him; fret not yourself over the one who prospers in the way, over the man who carries out evil devices! Refrain from anger, and forsake wrath! Fret not yourself; it tends only to evil. For evildoers shall be cut off, but those who wait for the Lord shall inherit the land. (Psalm 37:7–9)

> I can do all things through him who strengthens me. (Philippians 4:13)

> Put on then, as God's chosen ones, holy and beloved, compassionate hearts, kindness, humility, meekness and patience. (Colossians 3:12)

> The Lord is not slow to fulfill his promise as some count slowness, but is patient toward you not wishing that any should perish but that all should reach repentance. (1 Peter 3:9)

> Casting all your anxieties on him, because He cares for you. (1 Peter 5:7)

> And we know that for those who love God all things work together for good, for those who are called according to his purpose. (Romans 8:28)

Do not be anxious about anything, but in everything by prayer and supplication with thanksgiving let your requests be made known to God. And the peace of God, which surpasses all understanding, will guard your hearts and minds in Christ Jesus. (Philippians 4:6–7)

The end of this book, but the story continues.

Printed in the United States
by Baker & Taylor Publisher Services